HIEROGLYPHICS

Ronald L. Bonewitz

TEACH YOURSELF BOOKS

For UK orders: please contact Bookpoint Ltd, 130 Milton Park, Abingdon, Oxon OX14 4SB. Telephone: (44) 01235 827720, Fax: (44) 01235 400454. Lines are open from 09.00–18.00, Monday to Saturday, with a 24-hour message answering service. Email address: *orders@bookpoint.co.uk*

For U.S.A. order enquiries: please contact McGraw-Hill Customer Services, P.O. Box 545, Blacklick, OH 43004-0545, U.S.A. Telephone 1-800-722-4726. Fax: 1-614-755-5645.

For Canada order enquiries: please contact McGraw-Hill Ryerson Ltd., 300 Water St, Whitby, Ontario L1N 9B6, Canada. Telephone: 905 430 5000. Fax: 905 430 5020.

Long renowned as the authoritative source for self-guided learning – with more than 30 million copies sold worldwide – the *Teach Yourself* series includes over 300 titles in the fields of languages, crafts, hobbies, business and education.

British Library Cataloguing in Publication Data
A catalogue record for this title is available from The British Library

Library of Congress Catalog Card Number: On file

First published in UK 2001 by Hodder Headline Plc, 338 Euston Road, London NW1 3BH.

First published in US 2001 by Contemporary Books, A Division of The McGraw-Hill Companies, 4255 West Touhy Avenue, Lincolnwood (Chicago), Illinois 60712-1975 U.S.A.

Typeset by Transet Ltd, Coventry, England.
Printed in Great Britain for Hodder & Stoughton Educational, a division of Hodder Headline Ltd, 338 Euston Road, London NW1 3BH by Cox & Wyman Ltd, Reading, Berkshire.

Impression number 10 9 8 7 6 5 4 3 2
Year 2006 2005 2004 2003 2002 2001

CONTENTS

INTRODUCTION

Before we look at the development of the written word, and hieroglyphics in particular, here is your first lesson: *Don't panic*. Both Egyptian and Mayan hieroglyphics appear to be extremely complex. If we were to go fully and deeply into either, they are. But ask anyone who has learned English as a foreign language about complexity! For an introductory book, the highly technical aspects of both writings can be overlooked or shortcuts taken. Not only that, with Egyptian hieroglyphs in particular, the ancient Egyptians were no keener to struggle through them than you are. As a consequence, they created a number of aids to reading them that serve the student just as well today as they did 4,000 years ago. By the final pages, you will have a basic understanding of both systems of hieroglyphics, and you will be ready to start reading inscriptions in both languages. In addition, you will be able to write English words in both types of hieroglyphs. But within this book, you can do as much or as little as you like: you can do nothing more than use the tables of glyphs to translate yours and your friend's names into hieroglyphics. There are modern Egyptians in Luxor and Cairo who make a good living from doing just this!

It would be well at this point to make a distinction, in the first instance, between Egyptian hieroglyphics and Egyptian. Egyptian is a language, with all the subtleties, nuances, complexities – and inconsistencies – of any modern language. It is a major study in and of itself, as is any modern language, and impossible to cover in a short book. Exactly the same can be said about Mayan. Beyond that, both languages are based on the cultures in which they developed, and without an understanding of the culture, many of the words and nuances are meaningless when trying to translate. Egyptian comes from a system of thought somewhat closer to modern thought; indeed, it may be argued that modern thought is a direct ancestor of Egyptian thought. But the Maya might as well be an alien species from a distant planet as far as their ancient languages are concerned – *languages* being a key word. The Maya never achieved political unity, and many languages were spoken in the relatively narrow confines of the Maya world. In some places, peoples from one city were unable to understand peoples from the next. But, they all used the same hieroglyphs for the most part. Thus the Maya section is about learning the hieroglyph system rather than the Mayan languages.

This is a particularly exciting time for the new student of the Maya. It is only since about 1980 that real strides have been made in translation. There are numerous websites dedicated to the Maya, and with a little 'surfing', you will be able to keep up with the latest developments.

Happy reading!

Ronald L. Bonewitz
England, 2000

1 THE WRITTEN WORD

The development of writing must rank as one of the top three or four human developments, along with the wheel, the use of fire, and language itself. Writing doesn't just happen. Writing was invented to serve specific cultural purposes; it is a means of transmitting information, both across space and across time. The particular writing system that develops depends on the functions required of it by its users; a system invented to satisfy one purpose may acquire new applications. For instance, writing systems invented for aiding memory (how many new goats were born last spring?) were subsequently elaborated and used for communicative and archival purposes. And as with hieroglyphics, writing was not invented as an art form but, once invented, could serve aesthetic functions.

Linguists have abandoned the idea of the evolution of languages, with some languages ranking as more primitive than others; historians of writing now treat writing systems in a similar manner, as appropriate to the languages they represent; and, that widely different systems can function efficiently, given the particular language they are used to portray.

The earliest writing system in the world was the Sumerian script, known in its later stages as *cuneiform*. Its earliest stages of development, possibly as early as 8000 BC, derived from a series of small, distinctively shaped clay objects, described as 'tokens'. Some are shaped like jars and some like various animals. A number of them are found in clay 'envelopes', some of which have markings corresponding to the clay shapes inside. The theory is that the clay shapes represent agricultural goods such as grain, sheep, and cattle and that they were used as a form of bookkeeping. It is believed that tokens placed in an envelope might have constituted a record of indebtedness. As a reminder of the contents of the envelope – so it wasn't necessary to break open the envelope every time it was read – corresponding shapes were impressed upon the outside. It was soon realised that if the content was marked on the outside, there was no need for the tokens at all – the envelope could be flattened and the shapes impressed on it, their message simply inscribed into the clay. These shapes, drawn in the wet clay with a pointed stick, became the first writing. Eventually, the symbols became less picture-like and more conventionalised. The writing system takes the name cuneiform from the wedge shape of the strokes that form the symbols (from Latin *cuneus,* wedge).

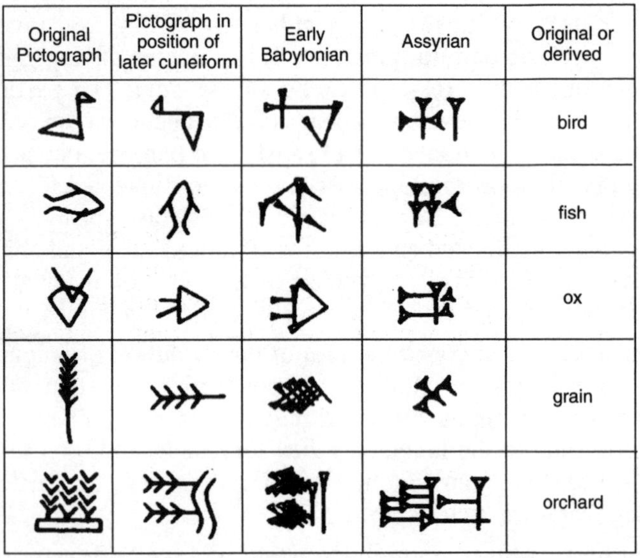
Original Pictograph
Pictograph in position of later cuneiform
Early Babylonian
Assyrian
Original or derived
bird
fish
ox
grain
orchard

Figure 1.1 Development of cuneiform script from pictographs to Assyrian characters

The next major stage in the evolution of Sumerian writing was to use a sign to represent a common sound rather than a common meaning. For example, the symbol for 'water' was also used to represent the sound 'in' because it sounded similar to the word 'water'. In English, we might use a picture of a cat to write the first syllable of the word 'category'.

By the 3rd millennium BC, the Akkadians greatly expanded the sound-equivalent properties of the script, and the Assyrians and the Babylonians, who both spoke dialects of the Akkadian language, were responsible for most of the cuneiform writing in a form known today as Akkadian cuneiform. It was along these same principles that hieroglyphics developed, at about the same time. It was originally thought that hieroglyphics was a direct outgrowth of cuneiform, but later thinking is that it was not. Such a relationship is improbable because the two scripts are based on entirely different spoken languages. But what most likely did influence hieroglyphics were the *principles* of writing established by cuneiform: the *idea* of writing itself, and the use of symbols to represent sounds – in particular, the use of symbols whose spoken sound is or resembles the word for the picture used to represent it.

Literacy set the major cultures of the ancient Near East apart from their contemporaries, opening up new possibilities in social organisation and in the transmission of a growing body of knowledge. There seems to have been no separate, illiterate class of nobility, as landed aristocracies sometimes were in other cultures. All high-ranking people, including kings, were literate. In all areas of social organisation, writing formed the basis of official activity.

Hieroglyphics

'Hieroglyphics' is not an Egyptian word at all – it is from the Greek, meaning 'sacred engraving' (*hieros* + *gluphien*). It is a writing system that employs characters in the form of pictures: its individual signs can be read either as pictures, as symbols for pictures, or as symbols for sounds. It is from this form of representing words or sounds with pictures that the Egyptians derived their name for their form of writing: 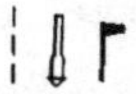. This word consists of three symbols: , , and .  is a writing stick, representing three sounds: m+d+oo, pronounced *medoo*, and is used to write both the words 'stick' and 'language'. The  symbol is a piece of cloth attached to a pole. These were erected in sacred places – especially temples and tombs – and indicated the presence of a god. The symbol is, in fact, used as the word 'god', *neter*. The three vertical strokes indicate the plural: gods. Thus the Egyptian word for writing was *medoo neter*, 'the words of the gods', or in English, 'gods' words'.*

It is important to distinguish between *hieroglyphics* and *Egyptian*. Egyptian was a spoken language; hieroglyphics was just one of three different scripts for putting spoken Egyptian into writing. In terms of a modern word processor, it is just a *typeface*, or *font*. Its equivalent in written English might be Old English – beautiful, very ornate, slow to write by hand, and diabolically slow to carve. And, all in capital letters.

In the strictest academic meaning of the word, hieroglyphics designates only the picture-symbol version of the Egyptian language. The word has been applied more recently to the writing of other peoples, wherever it consists of picture signs used as writing characters. It is always used to designate the scripts of the Indus civilisation and of the Hittites, who also possessed other scripts, in addition to the Easter Island writing forms, and in particular, the Mayan. Because of their pictorial form, Egyptian hieroglyphs were difficult to write and were used mostly for monument inscriptions and for other items that were expected to endure such as tomb walls, coffins, and tombstones, and for particularly sacred writings like the *Book of the Dead*. Hieroglyphs often served as decoration: sometimes, the symbols were painted with brilliant colours or covered with gold. Maya hieroglyphics were used for all these purposes, and for everyday' writing as well – the Maya never developed other writing forms as the Egyptians did.

The most ancient Egyptian hieroglyphs date from the end of the 4th millennium BC and are commentaries to the scenes carved on slabs of slate in chapels or tombs that were left as votive offerings. Many of these earliest signs cannot be read today, but it is likely that they are based on the same system as the later classical hieroglyphs. What they clearly demonstrate is that hieroglyphs were from the very beginning phonetic symbols, and that no development from

*Keen-eyed students will notice from later chapters that this appears written backwards – but the Egyptians always put 'god' first.

pictures to letters took place. Hieroglyphics was never purely a system of picture writing.

Hieroglyphics remained essentially unchanged for most of Egyptian history – nearly 3000 years – and the writings of the earliest Egyptians could be read and understood by their distant ancestors three millennia later. This is particularly remarkable when we realise that we can scarcely read English as it was written just a few centuries ago. This phenomenal durability was, in large part, due to the Egyptian beliefs about hieroglyphics, i.e. that they were a gift from the god Thoth, and that to alter them significantly would be a sacrilege. This benefited not only the Egyptians, but us today as we unravel hieroglyphs and the messages they convey to us across the ages.

Starting in the 1st dynasty (*c.* 2925–*c.* 2775 BC), images of persons often also listed their names or titles, the events of a significant year, and specifically designated personal names, places, and incidents. For example, a scene of a pharaoh's triumph usually included an annotation stating over whom he triumphed, and in what year of his reign it took place. It was about this same time that another major step took place: writing began to appear unaccompanied by pictorial representations. Among the first places this happened was on cylindrical seals, roller-shaped stones with carved inscriptions that were rolled over the moist clay of jar stoppers to prevent the sealed jar from being surreptitiously opened, and which, at the same time, described its contents. In the case of wine, within the inscription might be found its origin from a specific vineyard, its destination if part of a shipment, the official responsible for it, and most often, the name of the reigning king – the production of foodstuffs in Egypt was overseen by the government from a very early time, thus making most shipments 'official'. Indeed, this 'official' function of food production and its movement and storage – and the need to record everything connected to it – was undoubtedly the prime driving force behind the development of writing for non-religious purposes.

The development of Egyptian hieroglyphic writing came in several stages: at first, only the absolutely necessary symbols were invented, without a standardisation of their artistic form; in a second stage, easier readability came about by increasing the number of signs and by employing determinatives – signs that are not spoken, but that 'determine' the sense of the word to which they are attached. This is an excellent example of how the Egyptians made every effort to simplify the reading – and learning – of what was becoming a complex set of symbols. No one makes learning things more complicated than necessary, and the Egyptians were no exception – which is good news for the modern student of hieroglyphics. After a relatively short amount of study, the logic and pattern behind hieroglyphics becomes obvious, and learning them becomes much easier. Determinatives are a great aid in this, and are an important innovation – and one that we could make good use of in English! An example is the English word 'can'. It may mean 'able to' or 'a container'. The only way we are able to (can) tell which it is is by its context. Hieroglyphics eliminated this problem by adding another sign – the determinative – to tell the reader which meaning to use without having to work out its context. To continue the above example, if we wrote the sentence, 'The can can', meaning 'The can is able to', we would have to look further into the paragraph to discern its meaning – it might even be a dance! If we used determinatives as in Egyptian, (=) might designate that the word that follows it is a noun, the name of an object, and (+) might designate motion. Then if the sentence is written: The =can can, we can see its meaning much more clearly as we read it. The first 'can' cannot refer to the dance, because there is no determinative for motion, and it cannot mean the verb 'enable', because the determinative has designated it a noun. And likewise the second must mean 'able', because it has not been designated a noun; and, there is no dance just called the 'can'!

Determinatives can give us an insight into the life and times of Egypt as well. When the individual scribe wrote hieroglyphics, his choice of certain determinative often says much about his human experiences. When he writes the word for 'education' with , 'man striking with a stick' – the determinative for 'effort, action, or violence' – it throws considerable light on the teaching methods of his time! When the same determinative is used after the word for 'taxes', it conjures not only a clear image from the past, but one to which, even across the ages, many of us will identify!

Also during this second period, which lasted about 2,000 years, symbols were standardised, and few changes were made other than adapting the standard symbols to the artistic conventions of the time period during which they were carved or in some cases, written. In this second stage, about 700 symbols were used – although from the standpoint of someone learning hieroglyphics, only about 150 were regularly used – so, don't panic! The major use of hieroglyphics is also an advantage to the modern student; they were used primarily in inscriptions, most of which were in a religious and funerary context: temples, tombs, coffins, tombstones, and funerary objects. Because of the ritualised nature of these connections, there are standard ritual formulas which appear frequently, and which are easily recognisable with a fairly small amount of practice. Many of these concerned the activities and achievements of the  , the *per aa*, literally meaning 'big house' – a word which we recognise today as 'pharaoh'. As you begin to learn the hieroglyphic signs in the following chapters, it may at times seem tedious – bear with it. And skip ahead to Chapter 6 to see what you will soon be able to read!

In about 500 BC, the number of hieroglyphic symbols rapidly increased to several thousand, occurring as hitherto unused possibilities of the system were discovered. With the encroachment of Christianity, the knowledge of hieroglyphic writing was extinguished along with the ancient Egyptian religion, and knowledge of how to read them vanished. But before they did, they left a legacy in other forms of Egyptian writing that eventually lead to their decipherment.

Soon after hieroglyphics became widespread, a 'shorthand' version was developed. It is a form of writing designed to be written with a pen or brush rather than carved. In modern terms, it would be the difference between writing everything in block capitals, and handwriting. This script, called *hieratic writing*, received its name from the Greek *hieratikos* ('priestly') at a time when the script was used only for sacred texts. The structure of the hieratic script exactly corresponds to that of hieroglyphics, but the characters of hieratics were changed to the degree necessary to write them rapidly with brush or rush and ink on papyrus. Often the picture form is not, or not easily, recognisable. All commonplace documents such as letters, catalogues, textbooks, official documents, and literature were written in hieratic script. For the vast majority of literate Egyptians, hieratic script played a far larger role than hieroglyphics and was also taught earlier in the schools. Eventually, even religious texts were written in hieratic.

Around the time that Egypt was conquered by the Persians in the 7th century BC, for official purposes hieratic was replaced by *demotic*. The demotic characters are more flowing and joined and thus more similar to one another, with the result that they are more difficult to read than are the hieratic forms. It appears that demotic was developed expressly for government office use where the language was extensively formalized and thus well suited for the use of a standardised script. Demotic eventually evolved into a form known as *coptic*, and it was here that the earliest attempts were begun in decipherment.

The German scholar Athanasius Kircher (1602–80) started with the Coptic language, correctly surmising that the hieroglyphs recorded an earlier stage of this language. He also correctly believed that the signs recorded phonetic values. Unfortunately he was limited by the common Renaissance idea that hieroglyphs had a deeper symbolic meaning, and that their phonetic value was only a superficial part of the sign. This idea of deeper symbolic meaning hindered all efforts in the intervening years, until the discovery of the Rosetta Stone in 1799. The inscription on the stone was written in three different scripts – hieroglyphic, demotic, and Greek. In fact, the easily read Greek text stated clearly that text was the same in all three languages.

The stone was made known to all interested scholars, and important partial successes were made by the Swede, Johan David Akerblàd, and by the English physicist, Thomas Young, but the limitation still persisted that the hieroglyphs were symbols until Young proved them otherwise. But complete decipherment had to wait for the Frenchman Jean-François Champollion (1790–1832). His success in 1822, after long years of intensive work and many setbacks, was due to the recognition that hieroglyphic writing, exactly like the hieratic and demotic scripts derived from it, was not a writing system of symbols but rather a phonetic script. He started, as had his predecessors, from the names Ptolemy and Cleopatra which appeared in rings on the stone, and added the hieroglyphic spelling of Ramses' name, which was also known. He determined the phonetic values of the signs, and learned to read and translate a large number of Egyptian words. Since then, precise research has confirmed and refined Champollion's approach and most of his results – and underlined his remarkable achievement.

How Egyptians learned hieroglyphics

A scribe was trained in his first job by another scribe, and the children of important people could enter office very young – around the age of 12. The scribe's training was mainly in cursive writing, which was from the beginning the commonest form. Further instruction was needed for proficiency in hieroglyphics, which was read by fewer people.

In theory there are many possible writings of any word, but in practice words have standard writings, and are read as groups, not broken down into their components, as we do when reading an alphabetic script as in English. However, there was considerable standardisation writings, which make the script easily readable.

Astonishingly, many of the exercises written by Egyptian students – mostly from the schools for scribes – have survived. Their mistakes allow us to deduce that Egyptian writing was taught by the whole-word method rather than phonetically. It appears that the word was dictated aloud, and the student then transposed it into its hieroglyphic equivalent. The exercises show that when the pupil did not recognise a word dictated to him, he wrote it incorrectly; in other words, just as he heard it. Because he had not yet learned to spell by letter sounds, what he wrote on his papyrus was usually a word that sounded similar to the misunderstood word that was dictated, and whose word picture was familiar. In English, if we were to draw an outline around the word 'cat' without paying attention to its actual letters, we would have the 'shape' of the word. If we were to do likewise with the word 'cad', it would have a similar shape; if spoken aloud, it might be misunderstood as 'cat', and the outline drawn as such. When the word was seen by the teacher to be incorrect and the correct word understood and outlined, the exercise sheet leaves a clear record of the earlier mistake. So it is with surviving Egyptian exercises. But Egyptian students had it easier than their modern counterparts in one major respect: there are no strict spelling rules! Much more important than spelling was aesthetics – whatever spelling looks right is correct. How all of these factors come into play will be part of learning hieroglyphics in the following chapters. But from the standpoint of the modern student who is used to alphabets and letter sounds, the modern learning of hieroglyphics starts out with this method.

Abbreviations and cultural icons

There are a number of hieroglyphs that were derived from well-known aspects of Egyptian culture that were immediately obvious to an Egyptian, but without explanation, are a great deal less obvious to us. A classic example of this is the use of the 'pillar' symbol 𓉺 as an abbreviation for the great city of Heliopolis. The most venerated object in the Old Kingdom, which began in about 3100 BC, was the *Ben-ben*, which rested atop a pillar in its own temple in Heliopolis – north of modern Cairo – the centre of Egyptian religion at that time. It was said to be made from *bja* metal, meaning 'metal from heaven', and Egyptologists speculate that it was a meteorite, and some believe that it had a pyramidal shape, suggesting the shape to the Egyptians as having a special divine significance. It was, perhaps, the model upon which all pyramids were based. Thus every Egyptian would recognise the 'pillar' as being synonymous with Heliopolis – just as we might use a picture of the Eiffel Tower in place of the word 'Paris'. Another of these is the name for Upper Egypt itself sm^{c}*, symbolised by the plant that grew in abundance there: the sedge plant, drawn in flower in its symbol 𓇗 . It is an Egyptian equivalent of the English rose.

*The pronunciation of these marks will be explained later in the text.

Other hieroglyphs developed from common religious practices. For example:

	processional boat of Osiris	*nesemet*	'the Neshmet boat of Osiris'
	carrying chair	*3sir*	'the god Osiris'

Both of these derived from the carrying of images of Osiris in processions, and the ceremonial bearing of his image by boat down the Nile. The pre-eminent place of Osiris and his wife Isis in the Egyptian pantheon gives rise to another symbol: , *st*, the word for 'seat'. In the final judgement of one's soul at death, if one had lived a life of balance and harmony, the soul ascended to the stars, to the *Du'at*, located in the Milky Way, where one became 'an Osiris'. Thus the symbol is in effect, the 'seat of judgement'. Because of its association, its sound also becomes part of (or perhaps was originally derived from) the fully written out name of both Isis, *3st,* and Osiris, *3sir*. These spellings point out a discrepancy between the Egyptian spelling (and hence the pronunciation) of certain words – almost exclusively those of gods and certain pharaohs. These come down to us through the Greeks, who ruled Egypt from about 300 BC to its conquest by the Romans about the time of Christ, and who recast many names into a Greek mould. Modern Egyptologists have kept many of these, and they will be pointed out as they occur in the text, because in some instances they will affect the translation of inscriptions.

Getting started

Egyptian words are written without vowels – a, e, i, o, u in English. Presumably the words were so familiar that it was deemed unnecessary; aside from that, for inscriptions it would have required an enormous amount of extra carving, as well as space. Each carved or written word was, in a sense, an abbreviation. This is also in keeping with Egyptian practice in recording and writing down information: if 'it' was 'common knowledge', if 'everyone knew it', they saw no need to write it down. But the omission of vowels isn't a barrier either to reading Egyptian or writing out its sounds – as it isn't in English. For example, the English phrase: Gd mrnng is easily understood by most.

The problem comes in knowing how the words sounded when spoken. If you don't know the language to begin with, there is no way to 'fill in the blanks' when trying to speak it. Thus an Egyptologist using the standard convention of putting an 'e' where the vowels are left out can speak to another Egyptologist using the same convention, but to an ancient Egyptian, it would most likely be unrecognisable. For example, the Egyptian word *jst,* meaning 'now', would be spoken as *jeset* – by an Egyptologist. But speaking to an ancient Egyptian? One can almost hear the peals of laughter.

The writing of one language in the letters and sounds of another is called *transliteration.* Even in translating one modern language to another, it is impossible to reproduce exact sound equivalents. First, some languages use sounds that others do not, and some languages use sounds that are not represented by specific letters – the only way you know the sound is there is to learn the language. For example, in English we use a sound called a *glottal stop*. This is a sound that starts deep in the throat and comes as a short expulsion of breath. We do it without thinking about it – or writing it. The classic example is in Cockney, where written letters are often not pronounced. The phrase 'little bottle' is actually pronounced 'li'le bo'le'. So, how do you know it's there? Unless someone pronounces it for you, you don't. But in other languages, like ancient Egyptian, there were letters for sounds such as this. It makes a more complicated alphabet, but it allows the language to be precisely pronounced – at least when you know the spoken language and what the vowel sounds are that are left out when it is written. In fact, English used to have letters for sounds that are spoken but not written, but over the centuries these have been dropped.

Hieroglyphics were generally written from right to left – just as modern Arabic – unless there was a particular reason to write them from left to right. One such reason might be for reasons of symmetry; for example, if a hieroglyphic inscription appeared on the two pillars of a doorway. In this book hieroglyphs are written from right to left, because most inscriptions the reader will want to decipher are written this way. When looking at an inscription, it is easy to tell whether to read it right to left or left to right: the figures in the inscription face the direction from which it is to be read.

As aleady mentioned, hieroglyphics were written for their artistic appearance. As a sacred expression, the written word not only had to express divine concepts, it had to appear visually beautiful as well. To this end, words in hieroglyphics were always written to form a rectangle, even if it meant putting a letter out of order, or of writing them in several different sizes. Needless to say, this presents its own problems for translators – and students.

The basic structure of hieroglyphics

Hieroglyphics consists of two basic groups of symbols, *phonograms* and *ideograms*.

- A *phonogram* is any written symbol that stands for a spoken sound or group of sounds. In English, these are the sounds represented by the letters of the alphabet (A, B, C, etc.), or by syllables consisting of more than one letter (like the *sh* sound in shirt).
- An *ideogram* is a written symbol that stands for an entire word, or a concept (such as #, $, &, %, and so on).

In hieroglyphics, three types of phonograms are used: *alphabetic signs*, which stand for a single sound; *bilaterals*, where a single picture stands for two letters pronounced together (like the *sh* sound, as we just saw); and *trilaterals*, where a single picture represents the combined sound of three letters pronounced together.

There are two types of ideograms used in hieroglyphics: *logograms* and *determinatives*. A logogram is simply a picture of what it represents. A picture of an owl, for example, can be read as 'owl', or as the letter 'm'. A determinative is a symbol placed after the owl to tell you which of the two it is, and are not read as part of the word. Determinatives are also used to give an expanded sense of meaning: for example, a pair of running legs placed after the word 'walk' turns it into 'run' or 'hurry'. Placed in front of the symbol for 'house', they create the meaning 'to leave' or 'to go forth'. As will be noted later, don't be discouraged by the complicated sounding technical terms. When you read hieroglyphics, you won't classify them – you'll just read them!

The forms of hieroglyphs

Hieroglyphs in this text are all facing the right; that is, they are intended to be read from right to left, as most Egyptian inscriptions will be. This will take some practice to get used to the idea, but it comes naturally after a surprisingly short time.

Hieroglyphs drawn in this book are a mixture of both their carved and painted appearance. Actual carved hieroglyphs are often just outlines, but may also be carved or painted in more detailed versions. Artistic styles of the times also influenced how hieroglyphs were carved or drawn. In Figure 1.4 below is the symbol for the two-consonant *h3* sound, drawn as  in their Old (a) and Middle Kingdom (b) versions, and written in ink in the *Book of the Dead* (c) – second row, second from the right.

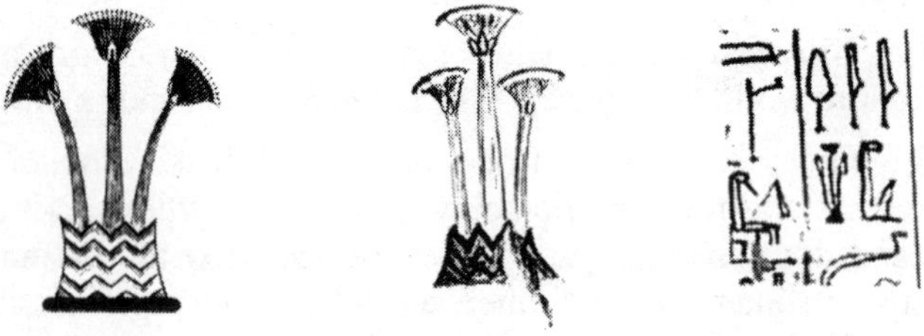

a b c

Figure 1.4 Forms of the *h3* sign

In Figure 1.5 (opposite) we see how various signs evolved over time, in their hieroglyphic, hierotic and demotic forms

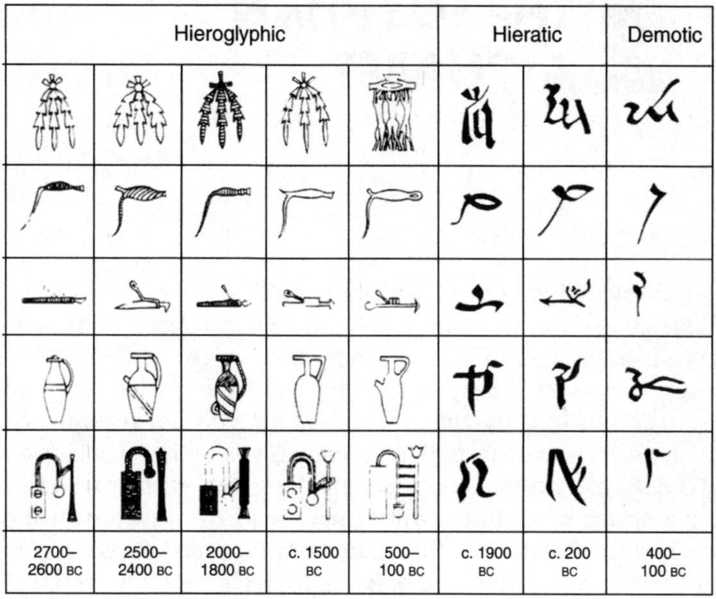

From G. Moller, *Zeitschrift des Deutschen Vereins für Buchwesen und Schrifttum*, ii (1919), 78

Figures 1.5 Changes in signs

But, in every instance, the hieroglyphs you will encounter in carved form will still retain the basic outline, and you will have no trouble in recognising them. Again, it is comparable to different typefaces in English – they all vary somewhat, but still retain the basic shape of the letter.

2 THE EGYPTIAN ALPHABET

In this chapter we start into the hieroglyphs themselves. Don't try to do these all at once, and take plenty of time: copy them out by hand – there is a 'shorthand' way of doing this suggested later in the chapter – so you will become familiar with them. Later, there are some exercises to start using hieroglyphics, both for reading and writing. You can learn as much or as little as you wish, depending on how deeply you wish to study hieroglyphics. This chapter will give you the basics so you can write names and English words using hieroglyphics: only a few Egyptian words are introduced. If you want to read inscriptions and other hieroglyphic writing, you will need to continue on through to Chapter 6. This will give you a good, basic grounding in both the hieroglyphics and the Egyptian words you are most likely to encounter. This will still fall short of a complete course in Egyptian, for the simple reason that there are possibly 1,000 hieroglyphs (no one has actually counted them!), and even Egyptologists have to look up quite a few of them. And, the study of Egyptian is a language course in and of itself – ancient Egyptian is as complex and sophisticated as any modern language, and is just as difficult to learn to gain fluency.

REVIEW

Hieroglyphics consists of two basic groups of symbols, **phonograms** and **ideograms**.

- A **phonogram** is any written symbol that stands for a spoken sound or group of sounds. In English, these are the sounds represented by the letters of the alphabet (A, B, C, etc.), or by syllables consisting of more than one letter (like the *sh* sound in shirt).
- An **ideogram** is a written symbol that stands for an entire word, or a concept (such as #, $, &, %, and so on).

In hieroglyphics, three types of phonograms are used: *alphabetic signs*, which stand for a single sound; *bilaterals*, where a single picture stands for two letters pronounced together (like the *sh* sound, above); and *trilaterals*, where a single picture represents the combined sound of three letters pronounced together. These are used much like syllables in English, except that one symbol stands for the entire syllable.

There are two types of ideograms used in hieroglyphics: *logograms* and *determinatives*. A logogram is simply a picture of what it represents. A picture of an owl, for example, can be read as 'owl', or as the letter 'm'. A determinative is a symbol placed after the owl to tell you which of the two it is. Determinatives are also used to give an expanded sense of meaning: for example, a pair of running legs placed after the word 'walk' turns it into 'run' or 'hurry'.

Note: Don't be put off by the technical names. They are useful for sorting out hieroglyphs for learning, but when reading, you just read them!

Transliteration

Transliteration is simply the action of writing the sounds of one language using the symbols – the alphabet* – of another. While English is an excellent language for expressing a wide range of ideas and concepts, the correspondence – or more accurately, the poor correspondence – between its written symbols and its spoken sounds makes it extremely difficult to learn. For example, say these words aloud: he, her, hem. Would you guess from their sounds that 'e' is the second letter of each? You would only if you knew the language. But written Egyptian is a much more accurate portrayal of its actual sounds. But where Egyptian would have a different symbol for each of the previous 'e' sounds, we only have one.

*In the strictest academic sense of the word, hieroglyphics is not an 'alphabet', in particular because it doesn't write out its vowel sounds. For practical purposes of learning hieroglyphics, however, it is close enough, and the term will be used throughout the book.

Because written Egyptian has symbols for many more sounds than can be written in English, if we are going to represent Egyptian sounds with the very limited English alphabet, we need to invent some English symbols to represent Egyptian sounds. These symbols are standardised academic symbols for writing Egyptian – transliterating – and are shown in the 'transliteration' column below, as well as in succeeding tables of symbols. They are made up by adding an additional symbol to the basic English symbol, and indicate the English pronunciation version of that letter.

Throughout the text, the hieroglyphics are written right to left, but the transliteration into the English alphabet is written left to right, as in English. This sounds confusing, but because we are used to reading English in that direction, it is actually easier in the long run. As you progress with your study, you will actually find it quite natural. But this is for later chapters. Here we will concentrate on the signs that can be represented by single English sounds.

REVIEW

Egyptian is written in consonants, omitting vowels.

Origin of hieroglyphic symbols

The sound symbols of hieroglyphics were often generated from the Egyptian word of which they were a part – usually the first syllable. They came in most instances from the spoken words for plants, animals, and objects familiar to everyone. Here are a few examples:

	*s*	from the word *sw*, length of cloth
	*gm*	from *gmt*, black ibis
	*r*	from *r'*, mouth
	*p*	from *pj*, mat
	*jr*	from *jrt*, eye
	*h'*	from *h'j*, appear (the glyph is the rising sun)
	*t*	from *tj*, loaf of bread

While many of the symbols are obvious from their appearance, others are somewhat less so. The last symbol is a classic example of this. Bread was baked in several ways in ancient Egypt, ranging from the familiar glob of dough heating on a flat rock, to elegant, cone-shaped loaves of extremely fine bread baked for religious offerings. Both of these types of bread appear as hieroglyphs, like '*t*' above. In the tomb painting shown here, we see preparations being made for the baking of conical loaves: earthenware pots being pre-heated, into which the dough was poured directly, and in which the bread slowly baked without direct fire. Conical loaves appear as hieroglyphs themselves, or as components of other hieroglyphs – those related to making offerings, or the actual act of offering.

The basic Egyptian alphabet consists of 24 single-consonant signs. Table 2.1 overleaf shows the single-consonant hieroglyphs whose sounds are pronounced as in English.

Table 2.1

Hieroglyph	Picture	Transliteration	Pronunciation
𓃀	leg	*b*	b as in *bet*
𓂧	hand	*d*	d as in *did*
𓆑	horned viper	*f*	f as in *fit*
𓎼	jar stand	*g*	g as in *get*
𓉔	courtyard	*h*	h as in *home*
𓇋	reed leaf	*ỉ* or *y*	(weak y)
𓇌	double reed leaf	*ỉ* or *y*	y as in *yes*
𓏭	*or* two strokes	*ỉ* or *y*	as above
𓎡	basket	*k*	k as in *kite*
𓅓	owl	*m*	m as in *met*
𓈖	water	*n*	n as in *new*
𓋔	*or* red crown	*n*	as above
𓊪	wicker stool	*p*	p as in *pin*
𓂋	mouth	*r*	r as in *rain* (trilled)
𓋴	folded cloth	*s*	s as in *sun*
𓏏	bread loaf	*t*	t as in *Tom*
𓅱	quail chick	*w*	w as in *when*
𓏲	*or* from the cursive	*w*	as above
𓊃	door bolt	*z*	combined *s* and *z*

Further single-consonants

There is another group of single consonants whose sounds are not English sounds, and are pronounced as indicated in Table 2.2.

Table 2.2

Hieroglyph	Picture	Transliteration	Pronunciation
𓄿	vulture	*3*	glottal stop, like the Cockney 'li'le bo'le' for 'little bottle'
𓂝	lower arm	ᶜ	deep glottal a – like trying to say 'ah' while swallowing
𓎛	twisted flax wick	*ḥ*	hard h – say 'ha-ha' sharply
𓐍	placenta	*ḫ*	soft h – like German *ich*
𓄡	animal belly	*ẖ*	aspirated h – as in Bach
𓈙	pool	*š*	sh as in 'shout'
𓈎	slope	*ḳ*	c as in cough
𓍿	tether rope	*ṯ*	sharp t – as in 'tune'
𓆓	cobra	*ḏ*	dj as in adjust

As we move out of transliterating English into hieroglyphics and start dealing with Egyptian words, these will become more prominent.

Drawing hieroglyphs

One of the most daunting tasks for the student is actually drawing the characters themselves. But you don't have to be artistic. First, practice by drawing each character in Tables 2.1 and 2.2 by using just a few lines that create a figure that looks like the hieroglyph – use it is a sort of 'shorthand'. The author's version can be found in Table 2.3, to give you a few ideas. When you are making up a block, first transcribe the name in these 'shorthand' drawings. You may need to do it several times to arrive at the most artistic block. When you have arrived at a 'final draft', then, if you are computer literate, you might want to scan in the formalised drawings from the text, and reassemble them in the computer. Or you can photocopy drawings from the text and use 'cut and paste' to reassemble them. And finally you can, of course, draw them out by hand. Here are suggestions for drawing the symbols in Tables 2.1 and 2.2:

Table 2.3

REVIEW

Hieroglyphics can be written facing either direction, but are usually written from right to left: the figures in the inscription face the direction from which it is to be read.

Hieroglyphics are arranged in blocks for aesthetic appearance. Each block comprises a word. There are no spaces between the blocks, and no punctuation.

Variations on the above rules

In addition to these basic rules for writing hieroglyphics, from time to time there were variations that depended primarily on artistic considerations:

1. Individual hieroglyphs could be enlarged or shrunk to make the blocks more artistically balanced. When this was done, the characters still retained their form.
2. The order of the characters in each word could be rearranged to make a neater block. But when the letters were rearranged, it followed definite rules.
3. Some characters could be written horizontally or vertically, again to suit the artistic requirements of the block.
4. In some cases, characters are left out entirely – a form of abbreviation.
5. There is no punctuation in hieroglyphics, and no spacing between words. But most words will be identifiable by the arrangement of the characters to form blocks.

These quite loose rules of writing hieroglyphics may make the task of reading them seem daunting, but it is easier than it sounds. Variation 1 will be encountered frequently, but because the character itself is unchanged, there is no problem reading it. Variation 2 is encountered on a fair number of occasions, but in most instances the appearance of the block will offer good visual clues. Variation 3 is found from time to time, but because the characters are unchanged, once you become familiar with them, it will present no problem. Variation 4 is a little trickier, but this occurs mainly in inscriptions that are part of a ritualised formula, and you will know from both the context, and the recognition of the standard formula itself.

In terms of reading hieroglyphs generally, in most cases they are not difficult to recognise in that almost all of them represent either a living plant, animal, object such as a vase, or a piece of equipment such as a plow. Because they are not abstract geometric shapes – unlike English letters – they are also generally easy to learn. They are not all easy to write, but don't worry if your first hieroglyphs are less than perfect – they weren't for Egyptian students either!

Exercises

Using the rules and hieroglyphs learned thus far, let's write out a few names, transliterating them from English into hieroglyphics. We begin with the man's name Guy.

Example 1 The name Guy:

1 First we drop the vowels: Gy

2 Then from Table 2.1 we find the letters that *sound* like the consonants

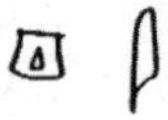

3 Remember they are written from right to left

4 After they are written, a final figure is added: the figure of a seated man, to show that it is a man's name. This is a *determinative*.

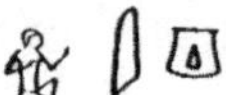

Example 2 The name Herbert:

1 As before, we drop the vowels: Hrbrt

2 As before, we look up the hieroglyphs from Table 2.1, and arrange them from right to left: trbrH

3 This now – to your new Egyptian way of seeing writing – becomes an awkward string of hieroglyphs. So the next stage is to rearrange them in a block

4 This works, but there is an even neater block if we put the determinative into the block

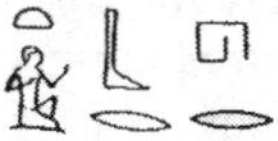

5 This is fine if Hrbrt is part of an inscription running horizontally. But suppose his name appears as part of an inscription running down a door pillar. Besides being written from left to right or right to left, hieroglyphics can also be written from op to bottom. Now we might construct the block as

6 This works as long as Hrbrt's inscription is on the left pillar, so all of his hieroglyphs face the door itself. But no Egyptian would turn his back on a door opening (for reasons of manners, not – presumably at least – for reasons of safety!). So if Hrbrt's inscription is on the right pillar, his hieroglyphs will be read from left to right, so they too face the door opening

7 And finally, if Hrbrt were pharaoh, his name would be enclosed in a cartouche, with the sacred knot closing its circle placed in accordance with how his name is written. In keeping with the rules of *abbreviation*, there will usually be a ritual formula placed inside or alongside the cartouche (such as 'son of Re'), but these will be covered in a later chapter

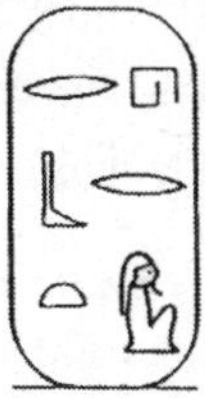

Example 3 The name Mary:

1 Follow steps 1 and 2 as above: Mry

2 For a female name, we add the figure of a seated woman – the *determinative* that tells us it is a woman's name

3 Again, the string of hieroglyphs is awkward, so this time they can be rearranged in a tidy block by *changing the size* of some of them

4 To write this vertically, the *order of the letters* might be rearranged to make a tidier block

Here are a few more determinatives that might be attached to a name:

	god (as in 'the god' Thoth – a title)		goddess
	official (as a title – Mary, the official)		child

There are a number of determinatives, many of which are explored in the following chapter. Most determinatives provide a sense of the words they are attached to, and are drawn from the activity or object portrayed in the picture. Here are a few more common ones:

> motion (walking legs) — army or military (soldier)
>
> the arch of the sky — grape vines
>
> eat, speak, emotion (hand to mouth: actions connected to the mouth)
>
> effort, action, violence (man striking with two-handed staff)
>
> The last example can also be show as , and both can be equally illustrated by just the arm itself, holding a stick.

Here are some other examples of words using determinatives. Note how you could work out the general meaning of the word just from the picture used as a determinative.

 *'3w,* old man

 *mhw.t,* family, household

 *pr,* go forth

 *^{c}n,* go back,'return

There are a fairly large number of determinatives, more of which will appear later. Egyptian teachers were as concerned about making writing as easy as possible for students, and as easy to read as possible – both served well by the use of determinatives. If we still spoke ancient Egyptian it would be much easier, but even so, in many respects it is a much more logical written language than English.

Two-consonant signs

This chapter introduces the idea of two-consonant signs, although they will be more fully explored in the following chapter. Two-consonant signs are introduced here because one of them in particular is useful for transcribing Egyptian sounds into English. Although the term 'two-consonant' is used, the author finds it more useful to think of them simply as *syllables*: single signs that incorporate two sounds. In many respects Egyptian is able to reproduce much more accurately its spoken sounds than is English. The English word 'her' requires three letters, one of which is scarcely heard at all. But the same word written in Egyptian could be first of all shortened to *h*r, and then written by a single sign:

 . So, the sign  would incorporate both the syllable 'her' and the word 'her'. Thus if we wanted to write the word 'hermit', we could use the single symbol for 'her' and then the rest of the word. Or, if we wanted to just write the word 'her' we can use the single symbol. The Egyptians did exactly the same thing. Certain symbols can be both sounds and complete words. How do we know which is which? When a single symbol is used as a complete word, it is accompanied by a *determinative* – just like various examples already noted. This is usually a single short stroke: | . Here are two examples:

	pronounced *pr*, it is the top view of a house, and with a determinative stroke added, it becomes the word 'house' –
	pronounced exactly the same way.

𓇳	the sun disc, pronounced r^c (ra), becomes 'the sun' when a
𓇳𓏤	determinitive stroke is added

Further notes on transliteration

There are hieroglyphs which are close in sound to vowels, and they can be used for them when writing English words and names, if you do not want to use consonants only. They are:

𓄿 for a

𓇋 or 𓇌 for i

𓅱 for o and u

𓃭 for 'l' sounds

For e, when it is unstressed, it can be left out. For example, the name Jed can be written *Jd*: 𓆓𓂧. When the e is stressed as in 'Marie', it can be written 𓅓𓄿𓂋𓇌, using the 'i' sound as an ending: *Mari*. Or:

𓅓𓄿𓂋𓇋,

There are two consonants for which there is no exact hieroglyphic equivalent: l, as noted above, and v. For v, use a 𓆑 *f*. The name Victor would be written *Fictor*, which is a close approximation. As with all hieroglyphics, translating them into English sounds is all a matter of approximation. When writing names, always write them as they sound, not in our often absurd English spellings.

Finally, you can enclose the name you have written in a *cartouche*. There are some blank examples at the end of the book. It is suggested that you photocopy these, and make several copies to practice laying out the hieroglyphs artistically within them. Cartouches can also be written vertically, with the hieroglyphs arranged from top to bottom.

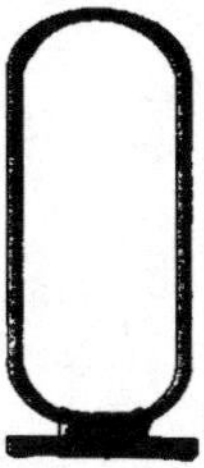

Figure 2.2 Vertical cartouche

Cartouches were used exclusively for enclosing royal names, and probably derive from a mystical symbol called the Girdle of Isis, essentially a cord around the waist, tied in a mystical knot – symbolic of the circle of fulfilled life. Although Egyptian is normally written right to left, the Egyptians *sometimes* wrote from left to right, so if you wish to write names or other English words that way, its not really wrong.

Exercises

The answers to all the exercises in the book can be found at the back of the book.

Translate the following names:

2.1  or 

2.2 

2.3 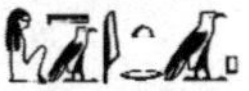

2.4 

2.5 

2.6 

2.7 

2.8 

Translate the following royal names:

2.9 

2.10 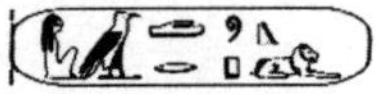

2.11 

2.12 

And finally, translate the following:

2.13 

2.14 

YOU CAN STOP HERE IF...

You only want enough hieroglyphics to write English names or words. The following chapters describe additional symbols for more complex sounds and uses, and Egyptian words and phrases are introduced. In fact, read on into Chapter 3 for just a few more symbols that will allow you to write more complete names.

3 SIGNS, WORDS AND DETERMINATIVES

In the previous chapter, single-consonant symbols were studied with the main purpose of transliterating English names and words into hieroglyphics. In this chapter, Egyptian words are introduced, and the more advanced hieroglyphics needed to write and translate them. This is not intended to be a complete course in Egyptian, but rather, to enable the reader to be able to decipher major portions of inscriptions. To this end, the hieroglyphs in the remainder of the book will focus on those usually found in such inscriptions. Other, more academic books provide a further resource for those wishing an in-depth study of the Egyptian language and the more obscure hieroglyphs.

The discovery that a single sign could represent a single consonant appears to have been a later discovery in Egyptian writing. The earliest forms of hieroglyphics were actually more complicated than they needed to be, but by the time this was realised, it was too late to start 'discarding' symbols. First, those who had only learned the 'new, improved' alphabet would be unable to read the older, more complicated one. Second, because hieroglyphics were used primarily for sacred writing, it is likely that it would have been seen as an offence to the gods to discard any of their gift of writing. The consequence of this for the modern student of hieroglyphics is that there are four additional categories of symbols to learn. Determinatives have already been introduced, although there are still a few signs to add. Next are signs that represent two sounds combined, then a few signs that represent three consonants combined.

Incidentally, there is no need to be discouraged by the complications of these theoretical categories for the symbols – they are helpful for studying them initially, but they have relatively little bearing on the actual reading of hieroglyphics. In practice, there is no need to decide whether a given hieroglyph is a bilateral or a logogram or a determinative – it is enough to know how it should be read and what it means. And, if you have forgotten how to read a sign, you can always look it up. All the signs in this text are arranged in tables at the back of the book.

This chapter contains a number of lists of signs. It is not necessary to struggle through them tediously trying to memorise everything as you go along. Look them over carefully, but mostly learn them by working with them. There are examples of inscriptions in this book, and there are plenty of Egypt books around with photos and drawings of inscriptions: take your lists and go through them looking for familiar signs, and learn them as you translate. And, as you will see, many of the signs are logical and have meanings directly related to what they picture.

Some of the sound signs can also stand for complete words, as in English: 'I' and 'a' are single letters that are words as well, and if we start a list of English syllables, the list becomes very long indeed. The same thing occurs in hieroglyphics, especially considering that in many instances vowel sounds have been left out. If we left out vowels in English, he, hi, and ho would all be written as 'h'; him, hum, hem, and ham would all be written 'hm', and so on. The only way to know which word 'hm' represents would be from the context, if they were used as words; used as syllables, you would know which it was by the word that the particular syllable was part of; for example, if presented with the words 'hmmng brd', it is easy to know that it says 'humming bird', incorporating the 'hum' syllable. Again, a similar situation exists in hieroglyphics, where spoken Egyptian would have been learned long before hieroglyphics were studied. But when they represent entire words, the Egyptians had exactly the same problem we would have – how to tell which word the syllable represents. This is done through the use of determinatives, introduced in the previous chapter, and expanded on in later paragraphs.

Hieroglyphs that are both words and sounds

In the previous chapter, single-consonant symbols were studied, two of which stand for words by themselves:

> 𓈖 *n*, pronounced *en* meaning to or for
>
> 𓅓 *m*, pronounced *em*, meaning in, from, or as

There is a group of symbols that are words but that are also sounds composed of two consonants.

Two-consonant symbols

Some texts refer to two-consonant signs as *bilaterals*, but here they will simply be called two-consonant signs; likewise the triple-consonant signs – often called *trilaterals* – are called triple-consonant signs. Table 3.1 contains some of the two-consonant signs you are likely to encounter. There are about 130, but these are the most common. This may still seem a lot, but the Egyptians probably thought the same thing – so at some point, another sign was added to two- and three-consonant signs to help simplify both them and their pronunciation. The additional sign is not pronounced – just as the determinative is not – and also like determinative, it helps to clarify the previous sign or signs. These additional signs, the fourth of the categories mentioned earlier, are called *phonetic complements*, and for the most part are signs you have already learned or will need to learn for other reasons. These will be introduced in the next chapter.

Among the symbols that stand for both words and two-consonant syllables, we find the following (Table 3.1).

Table 3.1

Hieroglyph	Picture	Transliteration	Hieroglyph	Picture	Transliteration
𓉻	wooden column	ꜥ3	𓁷	face	ḥr
𓁹	eye	ỉr	𓂓	raised arms	*k3*
𓌻	hoe	*mr*	𓎟	basket	*nb*
𓉐	house plan	*pr*	𓅭	pintail duck	*s3*
𓅨	swallow	*wr*			

The two-consonant signs in this table can also be used as complete words:

𓉻	ꜥ3	great or large
𓁷	ḥr	upon, on account of
𓁹	ỉr	do, make
𓂓	*k3*	immortal soul; the portion of the being that leaves the body at death
𓌻	*mr*	love
𓎟	*nb*	all, any, every
𓉐	*pr*	house
𓅭	*s3*	son
𓅨	*wr*	great

As you might gather from the pronunciation of the two-consonant signs given here (and those to follow, along with three-consonant signs), this is a good point at which to review non-English pronunciations, and the marks that designate them in transliteration.* Even with modern languages it is sometimes necessary to write foreign words and names in our own script, so that a reader who does not know the foreign script will have some idea of how the word sounds. Different languages consist of different collections of sounds, so it is not always simply a matter of replacing each sign in one language with a single sign in the other. Certain rules of conversion exist for writing the individual signs: often, a single sign is replaced by a combination of signs or by signs with special dots or strokes added to them to show that they are pronounced differently. These were introduced in Chapter 2, but they were less important in transliterating English to Egyptian. These will become more important as new Egyptian words appear: you may or may not wish to learn transliterated words by sound, but all standard texts on hieroglyphics use these standardised markings and pronunciations, and if you are intending to pursue this subject, they will be helpful in learning written Egyptian.

REVIEW

	*3*	glottal stop, like the Cockney 'li'le bo'le' for 'little bottle'
	c	deep glottal a – like trying to say 'ah' while swallowing
	ḥ	hard h – say 'ha-ha' sharply
	ḫ	soft h – like German *ich*
	ẖ	aspirated *h* – as in *Bach*
	š	sh as in *shout*
	ḳ	c as in *cough*
	ṯ	sharp t – as in *tune*
	ḏ	dj as in *adjust*

*Technically these little marks above or below the letters are called diacritical marks.

A further note on pronunciation

Studies of ancient linguistics – almost a separate science in itself – have allowed us to approximate the pronunciation of many words. As mentioned earlier, for everyday conversation, Egyptologists have adopted a simple rule to make the jumble of consonants pronounceable: they insert an *e* between each consonant. A word like *snb* is, therefore, pronounced '*seneb*', the word *nfrt* is pronounced '*neferet*', and so on. Certain consonants that have vowel-like sounds such as the symbols for *a*, *i*, and *u* are pronounced as those vowels, however the pronunciation that results from these conventions is, of course, totally artificial. A modern Egyptologist speaking 'Egyptian' would find it impossible to understand an ancient Egyptian and vice versa, but the two could communicate quite easily in writing.

Words using only the vowel *e* do not have a very attractive sound, so other pronunciations that do not follow these rules have long been used for many royal names. The king's name that would be spoken as Imenhetep by Egyptological convention occurs in older versions as Amenhotep, Amunhotpe, Amenhetep, and so on. The queen's name that would be vocalised by the convention is Neferet-iiti, but English speakers usually say Nefertiti, whereas Germans say Nofretete, neither form of which is correct; the Egyptian pronunciation was probably Nafteta. To add to the confusion, some kings' names also have Greek forms, known from classical authors, which are often used in modern books. For example, the name Amenhotep was written by the Greeks as Amenophis, and the name Khufu – the supposed builder of the Great Pyramid – was written as Cheops. Further examples of this can be found in Chapter 6.

Even so, in the tables and lists that follow, if you wish to pronounce the words and syllables as well as write them, you may wish to insert an 'e' as required.

Additional two-consonant signs

In later paragraphs *ideograms* are introduced, symbols that mean exactly what is pictured. Some symbols can be both ideograms and sound signs. A few of the common ones are found in Table 3.2 (two-consonant signs), as we will see later.

Table 3.2

Hieroglyph	Picture	Transliteration	Hieroglyph	Picture	Transliteration
	crested ibis	*3ḥ*		chisel	*3b* or *mr*
	stylised bowl	*3bw*		cormorant	*ꜥk*
	jabiru	*b3*		folded cloth?	*gs*
	valley	*ḏw*		bundle of flax	*ḏr*
	reed column	*ḏd*		fire drill	*ḏ3*
	water jug	*ḥs*		fish	*ẖ3*
	mace	*ḥḏ*		lotus plant	*ḫ3*
	sunrise	*ḫꜥ*		papyrus plants	*ḥ3*
	well with water	*ḥm*		herbs	*ḥn*
	tree branch	*ḫt*		plough	*hb, šnꜥ*
	bundle of reeds	*ỉs*		tree	*ỉ3m/ỉm3*
	spine with marrow	*rw*		three fox pelts	*ms*
	penis	*mt*		vulture	*mt*
	milk jug in net	*mi*		sickle	*m3*
	gaming board	*mn*		rippled water	*mw*
	canal	*mr*		whip?	*mḥ*
	pot	*nw*		guinea-fowl	*nḥ*
	ox tongue	*ns*		flying duck	*p3*

lion's hindquarter	*pḥ*	sedge plant	*sw*
water skin	*sd*	twisted cord	*šs*
arrowhead	*sn*	pool with flowers	*š3*
feather	*šw*	twisted cord	*šn*
sledge	*tm*	head in profile	*tp*
pestle	*ti*	duckling	*ṯ3*
lasso	*w3*	rabbit or hare	*wn*
ox horns	*wp*		

There are a few more common two-consonant signs that are not used in this book, but of which you should be aware. They are found in a table A at the back of the book.

Logograms and determinatives

REVIEW

Ideograms are symbols that mean exactly what they picture. There are two types of them: *logograms*, which are spoken, and *determinatives*, which are not. The same symbol can be used as a sound sign, a logogram, or a determinative. Where it is placed determines which of the three it is.

Determinatives are symbols that help explain and emphasise the meaning of other hieroglyphs, and are inserted after a word to give it additional clarity and meaning. They are not spoken.

Logograms are an important group of symbols that appear frequently and are signs that mean exactly what they picture.

Besides also serving as sound signs, some of them serve triple duty as determinatives. Where the sign is placed determines which of the three it is. Fortunately, in most instances it is immediately obvious, and it is unnecessary even to remember which of the three classifications it is called.

So, before moving on to logograms specifically, it is useful to look at determinatives again, and in particular many of those that also serve as ideograms when used by themselves. With a little practice, these can be quickly recognised, and translation is much simplified. When these symbols are used as determinatives, although they are not pronounced when attached to a word, they are still a kind of ideogram in that they mean what they portray. Because determinatives are positioned at the end of a word, they also serve as word dividers, since there are no spaces between words in hieroglyphic writing.

Determinatives were introduced in the previous chapter, as a form of designating whether a name is that of a male or female, or in one instance, that of a king or ruler. Aside from designating the gender of names, the same determinatives have a somewhat wider meaning. These are:

 which can also designate the occupations of men, or stand for the words 'I', 'me', or 'my'

 which can also designate the occupations of women

 which, aside from the names of gods, can also designate the titles of gods

Another function of determinatives is to establish the meaning of a word that is written in the same way as another word. For example, the word for 'old' is written *i3w*. But so is the word for 'adoration' or 'praise': *ỉ3w*. Why would seemingly unrelated words be written in the same way? Remember that the vowels are missing. The full words as spoken had totally different vowel sounds, which an Egyptian would have no likelihood of confusing. So, to eliminate confusion about which written word is which, a determinative is added. To the word for 'old man', the picture of a bent old man is added  ; to the word for 'praise' or 'adore', the figure of a man with his hands raised in praise is added  . Thus the words are written:

 *i3w* old man, or the old man

 *i3w* praise or adore

There is a further and even more dramatic example of how determinatives not only clarify Egyptian writing, but how it would be difficult if not impossible to read without them: the word *wn* (pronounced *wen*). This word has six different – and unrelated – meanings, and the only way to tell them apart is through the attached determinitive:

	open	determinative: a door
	light	determinative: the sun with rays
	Hermopolis	determinative: city with crossroads
	hurry	determinative: running feet
	to become bald	determinative: lock of hair
	mistake	determinative: small bird giving a negative meaning; can also mean weak, small, bad or evil

As we saw earlier, determinatives that involve the actions of humans are usually a picture of a person doing the action, or a related action. Words related to actions of the mouth – eating, speaking, and emotion – were represented by a person with his hand up to his mouth ; actions involving effort, action itself, or violence, is represented by a man striking with two-handed staff . Some determinatives make a subtle distinction about meaning in the way they are drawn. For example, the man in  is kneeling, indicating a more benign use of the mouth; the man in the determinative for 'to talk about' or 'accuse'  is standing, a more aggressive stance, representing a more aggressive use of the mouth. Table 3.3 contains some other determinatives representing human activities or states of being that will be encountered with some frequency, particularly in temple inscriptions.

Table 3.3

Hieroglyph	Picture	Meaning
	kneeling in adoration	jubilation
	official with staff	official as in 'official document'
	man building a wall	build (also an abbreviation for builder)
	man falling	fall, fell, overthrow
	fallen man with blood	enemy
	man with dagger	keeper
	royal figure	attached to names for the god Osiris
	mummy on bier	death, or lying down
	man with basket	work
	bound man	captive
	god with 'year' sign	The god Heh or million
	breast	breast or suckle
	penis	male
	legs walking backward	return, (to go) back, run away

There are other determinatives that are derived from nature, or from objects:

	duck or goose	bird (species of)
	trussed goose	goose (species of)
	falcon with human head	falcon
	sparrow	small, weak, pathetic
	ox	ox, bull, cattle (species of)
	desert dog	dog (species of)
⊙	sun disc	day, time
⌒	crescent	moon' or lunar-based event
*	star	star (name of)
	sand dunes	desert (name of)
	rippled water	body of water (name of)
	plant	plant (name of)
	cluster of reeds	countryside (name of area)
	scented pod or rhysome	sweet (name of)
	thorn	sharp or keen
ooo	grains of sand	mineral (name of)
×	crossed sticks	separate, pass by
⊗	roads within walls	town (name of)
	pustule	disease (name of)
	log with bark removed	scent or scented wood
	ointment jar	ointment (name of)
	lid or door	open

	sun with rays	light
	grape arbor	vineyard

Most determinatives will be used singly, but there is no reason that two – or more – cannot be used together. For example, both the 'man' and 'woman' determinatives are used together in the word 'family' or 'household:

And the determinative for force is used together with the plow in the verb 'plow' or 'to plow':

Logograms: Single-symbol words

As already noted, in many instances single symbols can stand for whole words or concepts. The technical name for these is *logograms* (word signs), and they are, for the most part, hieroglyphs you have already worked with. As an indication that these glyphs mean exactly what they portray, a small stroke (called, logically, a *determinative stroke*, because it determines whether it is a sound or a word) is usually added; for example, the plan of a house  can indicate the syllable *pr*, but with a *determinative stroke* added, it becomes the word 'house':

The sound-sign *sb3* is represented by the star-symbol , but when a determinative stroke is added, it becomes the word 'star':

Although the number of these logograms in Egyptian script is quite large, many of them are easy to recognise, even for a reader not used to hieroglyphics. In fact, many of the determinatives already learned can also be used as logograms (Table 3.4).

Table 3.4

Hieroglyph	Picture	Transliteration	Meaning
	kneeling in adoration	*hnw*	jubilation
	official with staff	*sr*	official (as in 'an official')
	man leaning on forked stick	*smsw*	elder, eldest
	soldier	*mš*^{c}	soldier or military expedition
	man seated with dagger	*ỉry*	keeper
	ox	*k3*	ox, bull, cattle
	sun disc	*r*^{c}	the sun or the god Ra
	crescent	*ỉ*^{c}*h*	the moon
	star	*sb3*	star
	sand dunes	*ḫ3st*	foreign land
	rippled water	*mw*	water, cleanse
	cluster of reeds	*sḫt*	countryside
	rhysome	*bnr*	sweet
	scented pod	*hḏm*	sweet
	thorn	*spd*	sharp or keen
	roads within walls	*nwt*	town

There is another set of logograms not used as determinatives that are either words in and of themselves, or in some instances the names of gods or goddesses written as with a single symbol. The ones most often encountered are shown in Table 3.5.

Table 3.5

Hieroglyph	Picture	Transliteration	Meaning
	official holding flail	*špsy*	dignified
	priest pouring libation	w^cb	priest
	arm holding wand	*ḏsr*	sacred
	arms with shield and axe	^{c}*ḥ3*	fight
	arms showing denial*	*n* or *nn*	added to words to form negatives such as: 'I did not', or 'it is not'
	water pouring from jug	w^cb	jug rests atop leg, symbol for '*b*'
	ox ear	*sḏm*	hear
	heart	*ỉb*	heart
	pair of crocodiles	*ỉty*	sovereign
	seal on necklace	*ẖtm*	seal
	standard with feather	*imnt*	the west
	sceptre	*ẖrp*	control
	pennant	*nṯr*	god (note inclusion of *nṯr* in next symbol)
	cemetery	*ẖrt-nṯr*	cemetery ('place of the gods')
	alternative for above		
	water pot with water flow	*ḳbḥw*	libation water and related words

* Another message across time: it is just like the gestures we use today. As, indeed, are most of the gestures frozen in time as determinatives and ideograms, clearly showing how universal and deeply grounded these gestures are in our basic humanness, whether as Egyptians 4000 years ago or ourselves today.

Table 3.5 – *continued*

Hieroglyph	Picture	Transliteration	Meaning
	palace facade	*ʿh*	palace
	shrine	*sḥ*	shrine
	grain measure	*šnwt*	granary
	fringed cloth	*mnḫt*	linen
	sail	*ṯ3w*	breath
	wall ornament	*ẖkrt*	ornament or diadem
	scribe's implements	*sẖ*	scribe
	road bordered by shrubs	*w3t*	road
	pattern of irrigation canals	*sp3t*	district*
	boat with furled sail	—	to sail downstream
	boat with full sails	—	to sail upstream
	seal on necklace	*ḫtmty*	seal bearer (a title)
Gods			
	falcon-headed god	*rʿ*	the god Re (or Ra)
	sacred ibis	*ḏḥwty*	the god Thoth
	egg	*3st*	the goddess Isis
	piece of flesh	*3st*	another ideogram for Isis
	falcon	*ḥr*	the god Horus**
	figure of Amun	*ỉmn*	the god Amun
	totem?	*mnw*	the god Min

*This is another culturally based sign: Egyptian administrative districts were defined by their agricultural uses, and in particular, by their irrigated lands.

** This is an example of an Egyptian god that has become known by his Greek equivalent, attached to him in much later times. There are a few more of these, to be examined later in the text

A snippet of grammar

Egyptian grammar is covered in detail in Chapter 5, but two useful parts are introduced here to make use of the vocabulary from this chapter.

Adjectives and genitives

Adjectives are words which describe nouns just as in English. In Egyptian, as in some modern languages like Spanish, they are written after the noun they describe. Where we would write 'green tree', Egyptians wrote 'tree green'.* Here are a few examples:

w3 mr great love

smsw sr eldest son

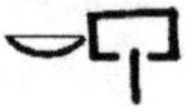

nb pr every house

špsy w^{c}b (the) dignified priest

This last example highlights the fact that Egyptian had no word for 'the' or 'a', and in translation, it is inserted where it seems appropriate, usually according to the context. Likewise 'eldest son' might be translated as 'the eldest son' since there can only be one. Note that in the answers to the following exercises, in some cases 'the' will make more sense than 'a', and vice-versa.

Exercises

Translate the following:

3.1 

3.2 

3.3 

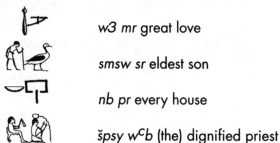

---

* Military veterans will recognise this format!!

3.4 

Genitives are nothing more than cases where two or more things that relate to each other are connected. In English this takes the form of 'the thing of the thing', or the 'thing of thing', as in the 'director of the company', or the 'Houses of Parliament'. It can also take the form of the possessive, ending in 's, as in 'Tom's house'. Genitives come before the word they are connected to, distinguishing them from adjectives.

	*w^{c}b ḏsr sḥ*	(a) (the) priest of the sacred shrine
	*špsy w^{c}b*	(the) dignity of (the or a) priest (note the different idea expressed here and in the use of the adjective 'dignified'

Translate the following:

3.5 

3.6 

3.7 

3.8 

3.9 

3.10 

3.11 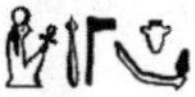

4 BUILDING VOCABULARY

Learning any language requires learning its vocabulary. This obvious statement can, fortunately, be modified when learning Egyptian. Learning the necessary vocabulary for hieroglyphics means learning only those words and phrases that appear frequently in inscriptions. Because these are often ritualised formulae, the necessary vocabulary is much smaller than the whole of the language itself. While every possibility cannot be covered in a book of this length, the most important words and phrases can be. It is suggested that at this point you begin to 'think Egyptian', and learn vocabulary by the 'whole word' method, rather than laboriously sounding out each letter individually. This is of particular benefit because, as you will see in Chapter 6, many of the ritual formulae are abbreviated. If you think about it, you do this in English anyway. When you read the word 'love', do you read it as l-o-v-e, or as the whole word? In fact, if you notice, the only words you actually spell out to yourself when reading are those words you don't know. Again, it gets easier with practice. In the meanwhile, there are just a few more signs to introduce.

Three-consonant signs

There are two groups of signs remaining that are, after all of the signs seen so far, mercifully small. The first of these are the signs that represent the sounds of three consonants. For the most part these also serve as words by themselves. There are only a few that you need to know:

	toes?	*s3ḥ*	
	dung beetle	*hpr*	'become, happen'

	heart and windpipe*	*nfr*	beauty, be beautiful
	bread loaf on mat	*htp*	offer
	adze	*stp*	select or choose
	oar	*hrw*	voice
 or 	rack of water pots	*hnt*	in front of', foremost

And now for some good news about two- and three-consonant signs.

Phonetic complements: The 'sound completers'

These are 'sound completers' that make reading hieroglyphic signs much easier: remember, the Egyptians were no more anxious to struggle with these than we are. They are particularly useful with the large number of tw- and three-consonant signs, and are single-consonant signs (the same ones you have already learned) that are added after a multi-consonant sign to clarify it. They appear at the end of the word and are a repetition of the sound at the end. Like determinatives, they are not spoken, but serve to make the ending clear; in effect, they are just a hint to the reader. For example, instead of writing the group *sw* as , you will often see it written as . It could be read as *sw-w,* but the correct reading is still *sw,* because the additional *w,* the phonetic complement, is only there to give you the correct pronunciation.

Two-consonant and three-consonant signs can, in fact, be written out in single-consonant signs. Often both consonants in a bilateral sign are 'doubled' by phonetic complements. For example,  *ʿ3*, 'great', can also be written as  *ʿ3*. But used as a word ending, or, indeed, as a logogram – a single sign standing for a word by

* This is the usual interpretation of this sign. How it comes to signify 'beautiful' is anyone's guess. The writer suggests that this is, in fact, a yet to be discovered musical instrument.

itself, in this case the word 'great' – it is often written as 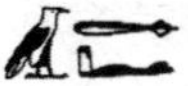,
as if were *ꜥ3–ꜥ3*.

Certain specific groups of signs tended to be used with phonetic complements, and if you follow on in hieroglyphics you will start to recognise these. For example, the name of the god Amun was almost always written with a final *n* as a phonetic complement: 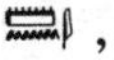, that is, *ỉ-mn-n,* to be read *ỉmn.* As mentioned elsewhere, this is one of the names that has retained its Greek pronunciation, Amun or Amon, even though the proper Egyptian spelling – and probably pronunciation – is otherwise. But, in general, there are no definite rules for their use, except whether the signs used could be grouped into artistically pleasing rectangles, although logograms are frequently supplied with phonetic complements. When you are translating, if you find a word in which the ending seems to repeat itself, you are probably dealing with a phonetic complement.

Terms denoting kinship

Kinship terms appear widely on monuments and in inscriptions – particularly those connected with the deceased. By naming all the deceased's family members – and often servants and other dependants – those named shared in the benefits of the offerings which the inscriptions made eternal. The key relationship usually expressed was that of the father to the son. The eldest son was not only the inheritor and provided the continuity of the line, but he was also the chief celebrant of his father's rites. Note that the words for the female relationships all end in  *t*. This will be explained further in the next chapter:

 *hỉ* husband

 *ḥmt* wife

 or  *ỉt* father

 *mw.t* mother

 *s3* son

 *s3t* daughter

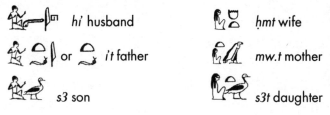

 *sn* brother  *snt* sister

 *3bt* household

Names

Because inscriptions are about people and their relationships – to others or to the gods – names are an important part of them. Royal names, as we see later, most often invoked the names of gods; in many cases so too did those of ordinary people, bearing in mind that those who were in a position either financially or socially to rate an inscription were hardly the 'men in the street'. Nowhere do we find an inscription to 'Semoset the ox herder!' Because the names of gods are frequently invoked – not only in the construction of people's names, but as gods in their own right in inscriptions – it is a good place to begin. It is also a good place to begin something suggested earlier: learning by whole words rather than sounding out the spelling. For reasons yet to be fully explained by Egyptologists, the internal structure of some of their names don't follow the expected rules. Also note that the names of gods are frequently written without the determinative for 'god' (see Table 4.1). Because everyone recognised the name, the scribe often saw no reason to add what everyone already knew.

The first name, Amun, also demonstrates the phonetic complement, as just described.

Table 4.1

Hieroglyph	Variations	Transliteration	Usual spelling(s)
		*ỉmn*	Amun or Amen
	 + ⊙	*Rᶜ*	Re or Ra
	–	*ỉmn-Rᶜ*	Amun-Re or Amon-Ra
	–	*ỉtn*	Aton

Table 4.1 – continued

Hieroglyph	Variations	Transliteration	Usual spelling(s)
		*Ḥr*	Horus
		*ỉs.t*	Isis
		*Wsỉr*	Osiris
		*Ptḥ*	Ptah
		*Zkr*	Sokar
		*3ḥwty*	Thoth
		*Zrḳ.t*	Selket
		*Ḥw.t-Ḥr*	Hathor (lit: the mansion of Horus)
		*Nb.t-ḥw.t*	Nephthys (lit: mistress of the mansion)

Royal names and titles

One the goals of this book is to enable you to read the names of the kings of Egypt. An Egyptian king had elaborate titles made up of his various names, titles, and epithets. An epithet is a word or phrase added to or substituted for the king's name. A modern equivalent, which appeared on coinage in many European countries in the last couple of centuries, was 'King, by the Grace of God' and 'Defender of the Faith'. Titles and epithets were part of the ritual formulae, and are covered in more detail in Chapter 6. Here, we focus primarily on the names themselves. From the Old Kingdom onwards, each king had five names, three of which are common on monuments; the other two are used less often. The three common names are the *'Horus' name* and the two names contained in cartouches – called the *praenomen* and the *nomen*. The less common names are referred to as the 'two ladies' and the 'golden Horus' names; because they are much less common, they are omitted here.

Remembering that the rules for writing and spelling are very flexible, in some royal inscriptions the symbols are arranged in differing orders and patterns from the arrangement of ordinary words, but they are expected in certain situations, and with a small amount of study, will be immediately obvious. There are a few situations for which the scribe's actions are totally unexplainable; these are a mystery to Egyptologists and still the subject of debate, and are thus omitted here.

The *Horus name* designates the king as the god Horus, the son and successor of Osiris, the god of resurrection and the ruler of heaven. The name is introduced by the falcon *ḥr* . For example, the Horus name of Senwosret I is:

	*ḥr ᶜnh-mswt*	the Horus Ankhmesut

The praenomen, or first cartouche name of Senwosret I is:

	*nsw-bity ḫpr-k3-rᶜ*	the king of Upper and Lower Egypt Kheperkare

The *nomen,* or second cartouche-name of Senwosret I is:

	*s3 rᶜ z-n-wsrt*	Son of Re Senwosret*

The meanings of Egyptian pharaonic names

The names of pharaohs inevitably had a symbolic religious meaning, and in particular, one that identified him or her with a particular god. When written in a cartouche, the name of the god always comes first, although often, grammatically speaking, it should appear later. This is because the god 'always came first' in all things. It is also because all the signs which follow it will always be facing it – it would have been the worst of manners for them to 'turn their backs' to a god. The following examples are written

*Collier and Manley, 20.

right to left in the Egyptian style, but the translated name is written left to right in the English style. Here are a few examples you will encounter in inscriptions:

1

Khafre

f	*kḫa*	*R^{c}*
he	rises	Re

May he rise, Re

2

Amenhotep

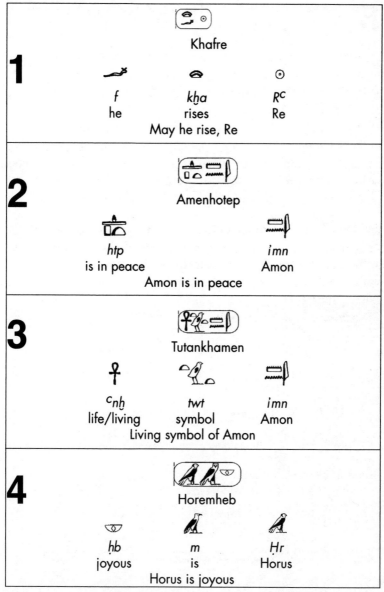

ḥtp	*ỉmn*
is in peace	Amon

Amon is in peace

3

Tutankhamen

^{c}nḫ	*twt*	*ỉmn*
life/living	symbol	Amon

Living symbol of Amon

4

Horemheb

ḥb	*m*	*Ḥr*
joyous	is	Horus

Horus is joyous

5

Hatshepsut

spsy.t *ḥ3t*

One who leads the venerables
or, First among nobles

Because most readers are more likely to be familiar with the historical names – mostly the *nomens*, the rest of the text will focus exclusively on those; but, when encountering an inscription, you will be able to work out for yourself the Horus name and praenomen simply by sounding out the name that follows the  and the  .* Throughout the 3,000 years of Egyptian history, there have been more than 100 rulers; it is impossible to list them all here. But, here are some nomens you may already be familiar with:

	*3h-n-ʿitn*	Akhenaten
	*Twt-ʿnh-i̓mn*	Tutankhamen
	*S3ḥw-rʿ*	Sahure
	*Snfrw*	Snefru
	*Mnṯw-htp*	Mentuhotep
	*Mni̓*	Menes
	*Ḥ3.t-špsy.wt*	Hatshepsut

* Having said earlier it is best to work with the whole word method of learning, this is an exception – the praenomens are less likely to be foreshortened or abbreviated.

There are other nomens you may have also heard – unfortunately there is a complication: they are not Egyptian names at all, but their rendering into Greek. Because no one was able to read hieroglyphics until relatively recently, the only record we had of the pharaohs was what was passed down to us in other writings, in languages other than Egyptian. This, for the most part, was Greek – Egypt was a Greek province in the last centuries BC. For example, the supposed builder of the Great Pyramid has come down to us as Cheops, and it is still sometimes referred to as the 'Cheops Pyramid'. Likewise the other two pyramids accompanying the Great Pyramid are known in some writings even today as the Pyramid of Chephren and the Pyramid of Mycerinus. But, these are the Greek versions of their actual names. The same is true of the name in an example seen earlier, Senwosret – known by the Greek name Sesostris. The following list contains their true Egyptian names, and other names that still appear from time to time in the Greek versions:

	*Ḥwfu*	Khufu (Cheops)
	*Ḫ*^{c}*=f-r*^{c}	Khafre (Chephren)
	*Mn-k3w-r*^{c}	Menkaure (Mycerinus)
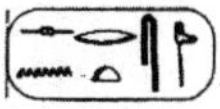	*Z-n-wsrt*	Senwosret (Sesostris)
	*R*^{c}*-ms-s*	Ramses (Ramesses)
	*ỉmn-htp*	Amenhotep (Amenophis)
	*3ḥwty-ms*	Thutmose (Tuthmosis)

When Egypt fell under Greek rule, hieroglyphics was still in use for sacred inscriptions; thus the names of its Greek rulers were transliterated into it:

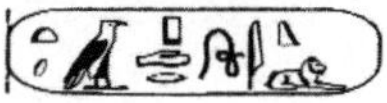	*Kliopdra*	Cleopatra

 *Alksandr* Alexander

 *Ptrwmys* Ptolemy

And, when Egypt was taken from the Greeks by the Romans, yet another name was added:

 *Kysrz* Caesar

Non-royal names

The practice of incorporating the names of gods into personal names was far from confined to royalty. Ordinary people – at least ordinary people who had sufficient status to have their names recorded in inscriptions – did the same. Here are a few of these:

	Ptahhotep	*ptḥ-ḥtp*	Ptah is content
	Satsobek	*s3t-sbk*	Daughter of Sobek
	Inhuretmakht	*ỉnhrt-nḫt*	Inhuret is strong

Other names invoked the name of the ruler, such as:

	Nebipusenwosret	**nb=i-pw-snwsrt*	Senwosret is my lord

And yet other names invoked the parent's hopes for the future well-being of their offspring:

	Nakhti	*nḫtỉ*	strong, vigorous
	Khu	*ḫw*	protected
	Senbi	*snbỉ*	healthy

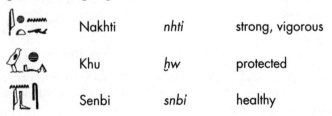

Titles

> **REVIEW**
>
> As you study the following titles, recall the genitive – the 'thing of the thing' case from Chapter 3.

As noted earlier, titles are frequently part and parcel of inscriptions. These take the form of formal titles, and epithets. Some titles which frequently appear are:

	*m-r*	overseer (lit: *imy-r*)
	*m-r pr*	overseer of the estate (or steward of the estate)
	*m-r st*	overseer of the storehouse
	*m-r* ms^{c}	overseer of the army
	*wb3*	cup bearer or manservant/ butler
	*wb3t*	cup bearer (female)
	*šmsw*	attendant

There are two titles that appear often, connected to persons who were close attendants of the pharaoh, and who therefore rated tombs and inscriptions:

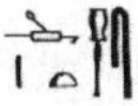	*smr* $w^{c}ty$	sole companion
	*ḫmty bity*	seal bearer of the king

There are several religious titles that also appear with some frequency, two of which are usually often translated simply as 'priest':

	*ḥm-nṯr*	servant of the god
	*w^{c}b*	pure one

Another religious title is:

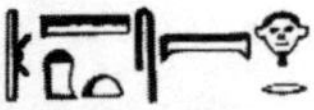	*ḥry-sšt3*	master of the secrets

These titles are frequently written omitting the determinatives. Note also that in 'servant of the god', the words are transposed. This is so that the god 'comes first'. The same sort of transposition also occurs in:

	*mỉ r^{c}*	like Re

where once again the god is 'put first', and in

	*rḫ nsw*	king's advisor

where the king is 'put first' before his attendant.

Endearment

Often a title holder is remembered with affection by the writer of the inscription, which again takes the genitive form:

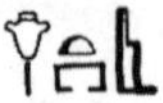	*st-ỉb*	literally meaning 'situation of the heart', i.e. affection or intimacy

It appears in phrases such as:

	*b3k m3^{c} n st-ib=f*	(the) true servant of his affection

Another word that appears both in affectionate rememberance and as part of names, is 'beloved': 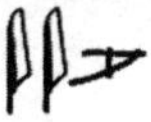 *mry*. Thus the phrase 'beloved of Amon' is written:

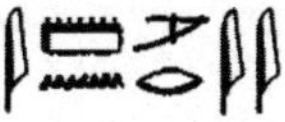 *imn-mry*

Remember, the god is always 'put first'.

'Beloved' is drawn from the word 'love' , often written without the determinitive, which can also mean 'wish', 'want' or 'desire', depending on the context. Note that it is another example of the phoenetic compliment, being written *mr-r*.

Exercises

Translate the following:

4.1 

4.2 

4.3 

4.4 

5 SOME GRAMMAR

In the previous chapters we have learned a few Egyptian words. How words are assembled into meaningful structures – phrases, sentences, and formulae for inscriptions – constitutes grammar. Those readers who have studied other languages will find a number of aspects of Egyptian grammar familiar. English is a peculiar language, being assembled in a somewhat higgledy-piggledy fashion from a number of other languages, and subjected to numerous modifications as it spread beyond the immediate area of its creation. Egypt was very well contained for a long time: geographic isolation was a basic character of Egyptian life, and the cultural attitude toward language – in particular the written language of hieroglyphics – kept it stable for millennia. The older European, Latin-based languages bear some resemblance grammatically to Egyptian, but these also differ grammatically from English. Fortunately, the rules of grammar necessary to read many inscriptions are relatively few; but, like any complex and expressive language, Egyptian also has complex grammar rules that are beyond the scope of this book. At the end of the book you will find recommendations for further reading.

Grammatical Gender

Nouns are words that refer to persons, places, or things. In Egyptian, as in most languages other than English, nouns that have nothing to do with men or women are either 'masculine' or 'feminine'. This is called *grammatical gender*, and in most cases there will be no obvious reason why a noun is one or the other – as in modern languages! Masculine and feminine words are usually easy to distinguish in Egyptian, because feminine words have a 't'

 as an ending, whereas masculine words can end in anything. To complicate things slightly, not all words ending in 't' are feminine – only *nouns*. In transliteration, endings such as this are usually divided by a full stop from the rest of the word, for example:

	*it*	father		*mw.t*	mother
	*sn*	brother		*sn.t*	sister
	*pr*	house	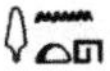	*nh.t*	sycamore tree

Some verbs can also take a feminine ending: for example,  'to do' or 'to make,' although the *.t* of the feminine ending often is not written, however.

In the previous chapters we looked at the kneeling man and seated woman figures as determinatives, but while we are looking at 'masculine' and 'feminine', it is a good point to look at the words for 'man' and 'woman'. They are:

	*s*	man		*st*	woman

There are no words in Egyptian for 'a' or 'the', so whether you are reading about 'a' man or 'the' man will emerge from the context.

Adjectives

Adjectives are words which describe nouns just as in English, and were introduced in Chapter 3. They must have the same gender as the nouns they describe and in Egyptian, they are written after the noun. As in the Chapter 3 example, where we write 'green tree', Egyptians wrote 'tree green'. The word 'this' serves as an example. When describing 'this house' – a masculine word – it is written:

 *pn* =  *pr pn*

When describing 'this sycamore tree' – a feminine word – it is written:

 *tn* =  *nh.t tn*

The plural and the dual

The plural of masculine words is created by adding a *w* to the word's ending, and *.wt* to feminine words. That said, however, it is often not spelled out phonetically but is shown graphically. A determinative of three strokes  is usually added, and most scribes considered this to be sufficient. This was especially so if leaving out the *.w* made a neater block of hieroglyphs. For example, the word for 'god'  *nṯr* can be made plural by adding the *.w*, but the block looks awkward. The use of the determinitive makes for a tidier appearance:

 *nṯr.w*  *nṯr.w*

The same can be applied to 'officials':

 *sr.w*  *sr.w*

On occasion, and only in certain words, three small circles can be used instead:

 *db.w* figs

A third option is tripling a logogram or determinative, as seen in the cartouche for Menkaure in the previous chapter:

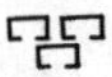 *pr.w* houses  *rm.w* fish

For things that come in pairs, there was a separate form, normally a doubling up of the sign:

 *c* arm

 *c.w* pair of arms (or two arms) or (both arms)

 *b* leg

 *b.w* pair of legs (or both legs)

There is another plural indicated by the inclusion of both the male and female determinatives, that applies to groups of mixed persons: first, the word 'people':

 *rmṯ.w* people

 *3bt* family (note that the word does not have a *.w* ending, as it is a plural in and of itself. It would acquire that ending if it became families).

Genitives: Connections of association

As introduced in Chapter 3, genitives are nothing more than cases where two or more things that relate to each other are connected. As noted, in English this takes the form of 'the thing of the thing', or the 'thing of thing', as in the 'director of the company', or the 'Houses of Parliament'. It can also take the form of the possessive, ending in 's, as in 'Tom's house'. The word 'of' does not actually appear, and is implied by position and context:

 *b3k. nsw* servant of the king

 *nb.t pr* mistress of the house

 *s3 dbỉ* son of Debi (a man's name)

There are two terms, occuring in inscriptions, that are titles of gods:

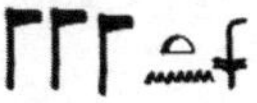 *nsw.t nṯr.w* king of the gods

 *nb ns.wt* lord of thrones

 *nb p.t* lord of heaven

Other associations express broad terms that translators tend to use a single word to represent; for example:

 *3w ib* 'wideness of the heart', i.e. happy

This is a classic example of transposing modern western thinking onto eastern thinking, which still retains much of the same belief as in ancient times. The heart was considered the seat of the soul, and at the end of life, the Egyptian soul was subjected to 'the weighing of the heart', wherein the deceased's heart was weighed against *Ma'at*, which symbolised the whole of 'right living'. This included one's duties to one's family, to one's self, to the state and to society generally, and to the gods. It also included personal fulfilment, and general contentment with one's lot in life. If weighed favourably against Ma'at, the deceased was elevated to a place in the heavens to become a companion of Osiris, and was him or herself entitled to become 'an Osiris'. Thus 'wideness of the heart' encompassed a great deal more than just 'happy'. Language is always an expression of the culture within which it grows; thus although we can translate Egyptian words, a much deeper understanding of the culture is necessary before we can understand their *meaning*. It is a task largely unfulfilled by Egyptologists, who are mostly westerners. Perhaps one of the readers of this book will feel motivated to undertake this hugely fulfilling task – one that would truly bring 'wideness of the heart'.

Suffixes

A suffix is a short word that is attached to the end of other words, corresponding in Egyptian to our personal pronouns I, you, he, she, and so on. The ones you will see the most often are represented by symbols you learned in Chapter 2, and are:

 = *k* you

 = *f* he

 = *s* she

'I' becomes a bit more complex. For part of the time 'I' was designated by the same figure as the determinitive:

 if the speaker or writer is a man

 if the speaker or writer is a woman

 if the speaker or writer is a god

For the remainder of the time, it usually appears as:

'Usually' because in cases where the writer or speaker is apparent – such as when a carved or painted image of the person is present – it was sometimes omitted. This form appears frequently in inscriptions, and when you see it, you can be sure the writer or speaker is saying 'I did/said so-and-so.'

Let's look at some examples of the use of suffixes, expressed in transliteration as =. Note that they take the 'thing of thing' form, as above: 'your wife' = the 'wife of you'; 'she hears' = the 'hearing of her'.

1 When attached to a noun, the suffix indicates possession:

	wife	*hmt*
	your wife	*hmt=k*
	his house	*pr=f*
 or 	my son	*s3=i* (female speaker or writer)
	her heart	*ib=s*

2 When attached to a verb, it forms a particular type of form referred to as a *sḏm=f* (pronounced *sejemef*) configuration. This comes from the form taken by the verb *sḏm*, 'hear'. It is the configuration of a large number of verbs, which all have the same general appearance when written, making their recognition easier:

	*sḏm=f*	he hears
	*sḏm=s*	she hears
	*sḏm=k*	you hear
	*dỉ=s*	she gives
	*ỉr=f*	he makes

For the 'I', we find the two forms, for both the possessive and the verb forms:

	or		*ḥmt=ỉ*	my wife
	or		*hỉ=ỉ*	my husband
	or	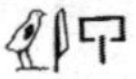	*pr=ỉ*	my house
	or		*sḏm=ỉ*	I hear
	or		*ỉ=ỉ*	I give

Tenses

The Egyptian indication of tenses is actually quite complex and beyond the scope of this book. However, the past tense is often used in inscriptions, in that they are usually a recounting of the life and/or deeds of the person featured. The past is indicated by the addition of an 'n' to the verb, which is called a *sḏm.n=f* form (pronounced *sejemenef*). Thus the above verbs become:

	*sḏm.n=f*	he heard
	*sḏm.n=s*	she heard
	*sḏm.n=k*	you heard
	*dỉ.n=s*	she gave

	*ir.n=f*	he made
 or 	*sḏm.n=i*	I heard (female listener)
 or 	*di.n=i*	I gave

There is another reading of the *sḏm=f* form that can only be deduced from the context: in some cases they can also express a wish. It is written exactly as the present tense, but in this case the suffix becomes the subject. For example:

 *ᶜnḫ=k* can be read as 'you live', or 'may you live'

 *ᶜnḫ=s* can be read as 'she lives', or 'may she live'

 *di=f* can be read as 'he gives', or 'may he give'

A common expression in this form is found in funerary inscriptions and on tomb offerings:

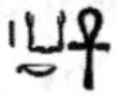	*ᶜnḫ k3=k*	May your ka live!

Another is:

	*iry=k hh.w rnp.wt*	May you achieve millions of years!

This expression is made up of:

	*iry=k*	May you achieve (lit: 'make')
	*ḥḥ.w*	millions (the ideogram for the god *Heb* *ḥḥ* is also the symbol for 'million'; the determinatives make it plural
	*rnp.wt*	of years (the symbol , a notched palm, is the ideogram for 'year')

The Negative

From time to time, the writer or speaker wishes the hearer or reader *not* to do something. In this case the negative , *nn* is added to the *sḏm=f* form:

 *ḥkr* hunger (note the 'bad thing' determinitive!)

 *ḥkr=k* you hunger

 *nn ḥkr=k* may you not hunger, or you will not hunger

This form is also used as an imperative, as a command:

 *h3b=k* send

 *nn h3b=k* you may not/will not send

Prepositions

The word 'preposition' literally means 'pre-posed'; that is, 'put before'. These are words like 'in', 'with', 'from', 'by'. They indicate directions ('towards'), how things are done ('by'), accompaniment ('with'), and so on. As in English, they tend to be short words:

 *m* in, from, as, with

 *r* at, towards people

 n for, towards a place

 *hn^c* with

 *in* by

 *n dbi* for Debi

 *hn^c dbi* with Debi

 *m pr* in the house

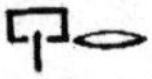 *r pr* to the house

Exercises

Translate the following:

5.1 

5.2 

5.3 

5.4 

5.5 

6 INSCRIPTIONS

As noted, names and titles form a large portion of the hieroglyphic inscriptions you are likely to encounter. Museums display statuary, monuments, and coffins, but only portions of written documents – most of which are in hieratic or demotic anyway. For the most part, inscriptions only occur for persons of some substance: priests, officials, master craftsmen, and, of course, royalty – in other words, people who had titles of some sort. And, because hieroglyphics were used as part of ritual, they themselves become ritualised in the prayers, offerings, and formulae that are written in them, many of which appear in abbreviated form. But just as we easily recognise RIP on a modern tombstone, so too did the ancient Egyptians easily recognise those abbreviated formulae. With a small amount of practice, they are just as easily recognisable today to the student of hieroglyphics. By learning relatively few of these, you will be able to read a significant portion of the inscriptions you are likely to encounter.

The King Bee

Two of the titles of the pharaohs which appear in most inscriptions are: *ny soot*, 'he of the reed', or 'he who belongs to the reed', and *bit*, 'he of the bee'. *Ny soot*, is used when referring to the king of Upper Egypt, the southern half of Egypt, and *bit* when referring to the king of Lower Egypt, the northern half.

The first of these is composed of, the sedge plant – a form of reed – pronounced *soot*, and composed of the sounds + + , meaning 'reed'; the sign, pronounced *ny*, is added to make it possessive (covered in a later chapter). The reed was one of the single most useful items available to the Egyptians, and was used to make everything from sandals to roofing. The pharaoh was therefore equated to this essential material – in essence totally interwoven with the lives of his people.

The second phrase , *bit*, may seem a strange title for the might of a pharaoh, but when we realise that Egypt was (and still is) awash with flowers of all descriptions, the honey produced must have been as exotic in flavour as it was in abundance. Surprisingly though, it was used less as a food and a sweetener than as a medication. Flowers were themselves held in high esteem, and the intermediary – the bee – took on a mystical significance. *Bit* was also the root word used to write 'the fine character' and 'a person of quality'. From this, it is not too hard to see how the pharaoh became associated with such a magical creature. These titles and others that regularly appear in inscriptions are explored further in Chapter 6.

Both halves of Egypt came under a single ruler fairly early on, and the two titles were combined. The new title was abbreviated somewhat, and written as:

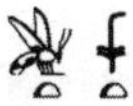 *(n)sw.t-bi.t*

The praenomen introduced by this title, and written outside the cartouche, read as 'King of Upper and Lower Egypt'. The title is actually a bit closer in meaning to 'king of the dualities', a recognition of the dualities which composed the Egyptian world: Upper and Lower Egypt; desert and the rich abundance of the Nile Valley; the human and the divine.

The nomen was introduced by another title, also written outside the cartouche: 'son of Re'; ie, 'son of the sun god Re (or Ra)', meaning the heir of the sun-god on earth. It was written as:

 *z3-Rᶜ*

The nomen was usually the birth name of the king before he became king, and is the name by which kings are identified by historians. It was, as in the case of the Ramessides for example, a dynastic name, shared with other pharaohs: Ramesses I, Ramesses II, and so on. The numbers after the names are purely a modern addition, and do not appear in ancient inscriptions.

Good wishes for the pharaoh

A phrase commonly appended to the pharaoh's name is often rendered in translation to mean 'Life, health, and strength', the wishes one gives to the pharaoh so that he or she has all the attributes necessary for a successful reign. It is seen abbreviated in some texts as LHS – a considerable oversimplification. In hieroglyphics it is also an abbreviation, reading:

It is made up from the following components:

The *ᶜnḫ* meaning life

The *ḏ3* the fire drill, from the word *oodja*, symbolising the words intact, safe, prosperous, and healthy

The *s* , and abbreviation of *snb*, *seneb*, meaning in good health

Another good wish that often accompanies the pharaoh's inscription is:

It is constructed from:

ḏt	*mi*	*Re*	*ᶜnḫ*	*di͗*
eternally	like	Re	life	give (may he be given)

May he be given eternal life (or life eternally) like Re

Again note that the position of Re is not grammatically correct – his name, out of respect, must come beforehand. These formulae should be read as a whole, and not as their individual grammatical parts. Also note that the sign for 'give' in this and some of the following inscriptions is , a form interchangeable with the  sign used in Chapter 5. This sign tends to be used where it is more artistically pleasing. A typical inscription using several of these elements looks like this:

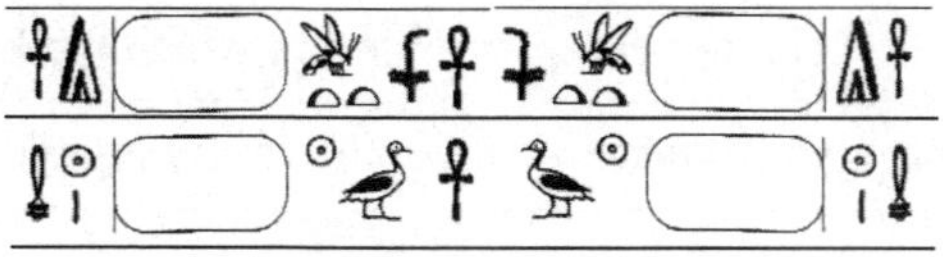

The offering formula

The various formulae are more or less fixed combinations of words, which are in turn abbreviated. It is worth repeating: read them as a whole, without trying to understand their internal grammar. The offering formula is a classic example of this, found virtually everywhere in museums throughout the world and on Egyptian monuments. Learning its elements puts you well down the road to reading inscriptions, hence we will go through those elements in detail.

The offering formula links the successful performance of official functions in royal service and ethical behaviour in life to increased status in death. This allowed the deceased to be commemorated by memorial inscriptions and funerary monuments, and also allowed the deceased to partake of the offerings presented to the deities in the major cult temples in the name of the king.

Its second function was related to the private, family-based aspects of offerings, which could be either physical (offering of food, drink and goods for instance) or verbal (for example, utterance of the offering formula). It was believed that these offerings could be sustained in perpetuity if presented in pictorial and verbal form. People visiting the tomb or passing by the stela would read the offering formula aloud, thus reinforcing its eternal production of the offering.

It consisted of three main components:

1 Who is making the offering and the god (and the god's titles) to whom its being made.

2 The type of offering, and what is being offered.

3 A statement that the offering is for the *ka*, the eternal spirit, of the deceased.

An exercise at the end of this chapter – from an actual inscription – will draw all three parts together. The first part begins:

	ḥtp-di-nsw	an offering which the king gives

This is an abbreviation made up from the following elements:

	from		*nsw*	king
	from		*ḥtp*	an offering
			di	give

This part of the formula was then followed by the name and titles of the god to whom the offering was being made – usually Osiris, although others do appear. Because there are variations on this, it will be covered after the remaining two parts of the formula.

The second part begins with 'so that he may give',  (see Chapter 5) followed by the type of offering, and ends with a list of what is being offered.

The next element of the second part describes the type of offering, most often a voice offering. It is based on the abbreviation:

This is made up from:

	from		*prt*	a going forth
	from		*ḫrw*	voice
	from		*t*	bread
	from		*ḥnḳt*	beer

Bread and beer are always depicted as part of the offering formula, whether they are actually part of the offering or not. The entire block is read as 'a voice offering'. It is sometimes written with the determinative 'offering':

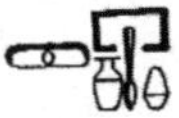

The items being offered in the formula are often abbreviated also. Some of these are: , from *t*, bread, and from *ḥnḳt*, beer, as above, when they are actually part of the offering, and:

	or 	*mnḫt*	linen		or 	*k3*	ox
	or 	*3pd*	fowl		or 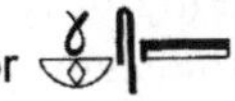	*šs*	alabaster

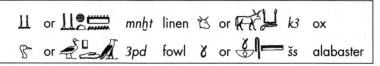

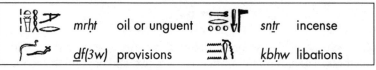

Other offerings tended to be spelled out in full:

	*mrḥt*	oil or unguent		*snṯr*	incense
	*ḏf(3w)*	provisions	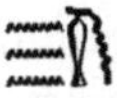	*ḳbḥw*	libations

There are three other phrases attached to the actual offering. The first is a ritual numbering, a symbolic 'thousand' that might be understood as 'lots and lots of!', written *ḫ3* 'thousand' or 'thousand of'. When the sign literally means a thousand, it is accompanied by a determinative stroke. Thus the following would read as:

 a thousand (of) ox and fowl

Often the 'offering' portion is itself abbreviated. rather than list 'a thousand of', 'a thousand of', 'a thousand of', only one 'thousand of' sign is used, followed by the entire list of offerings:

At the end of the inventory of offerings, either combined with it or below in a separate block, the following phrases are usually appended:

 'everything good and pure'

This, too, is an abbreviation, made from the following words (again reading from left to right). Remember that words like 'thing', feminine nouns, require a *t* ending from all the other words which describe it, and that in Egyptian, adjectives come after the nouns they describe:

w^{c}*b.t*	*nfr.t*	*nb.t*	*ḫt*
pure	good	every	thing

The  sign in the word 'thing' is a determinative used to indicate abstract ideas. Because a 'thing' is not a specific object, but a generalised term for any object, it is an abstraction.

In that this offering is being made to a god, one would not wish to offer anything that is not 'good and pure'. Likewise, the phrase that follows it says why it is being offered: 'on which a god lives'.It is written as:

 ^{c}*nḫt nṯr im*

This phrase is always presented in this form, and should be read as a whole. The internal grammar is complex, and beyond the scope of this book. Thus the entire phrase reads 'everything good and pure on which a god lives'.

The third part of the formula is the deceased recipient of the offering; or, more accurately, the eternal soul, the *ka*, is the intended recipient. There are two forms of part three, that ocurred at different times, and for a short period, *both* of these were used:

 *n k3 n* for the ka of

or

 *im3h(w)* honoured or venerated

The last is an abbreviation, the full spelling of which is:

 for a man, and  for a woman

Following whichever of these is present, you will find the name of the deceased, usually with his or her title (see the following paragraphs), and often ending with the epithet 'true of voice', meaning that they were judged innocent in the court of the dead. This is sometimes translated as 'the justified':

 *m3*^{c}*-hrw* true of voice, or the justified

These signs can also be written vertically: . These are both an abbreviation of , and sometimes appear as .

Osiris and his titles

Gods and their titles form an important portion of all inscriptions, not just the offering formula. As noted earlier, offerings are most often made to Osiris, the Christ-like resurrection figure of Egyptian mythology, but it is sometimes made to other gods. When a god's name appears in the offering formula, what follows are his or her titles. Since the god Osiris is the most likely to be the recipient of the offering, his full name and titles are given. There are variant spellings for most gods, and they are shown in the list following Osiris. Why the spellings of the names appear as they do is a matter of debate:

 or  or  or  *3sir* Osiris

Because Osiris was the pre-eminent god, over the centuries he accumulated a number of titles, one or more of which may appear. His principal title was 'lord of Djedu'. Note that Djedu and Abydos are both written with the determinative for 'city' . Both were actual places – Abydos is about 50 miles north of modern Luxor – and both had major shrines to Osiris where the rituals of his Mysteries were acted out at important ceremonial occasions. This has a modern equivalent in the Passion Plays acted out at Easter in some European countries. It was also thought to be the place of his actual tomb. Thus his principle title is 'lord of Abydos':

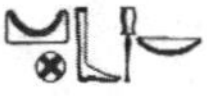 *nb 3bdw* 'lord of Abydos'

In his next title, the sign for lord *nb* remains the same, but the spelling of Djedu varies from inscription to inscription:

 or  or  or  *ḏdw* Djedu

There is another title frequently appearing in the offering formula, that represents Osiris' position as the ruler of 'heaven' – the realm of the dead, located in the west of the setting sun, and meaning 'the one who is foremost of the westerners', Khentyimentu:

 *ḫnty-ỉmntw* Khentyimentu

There is one further title for Osiris that is used on occasion in the offering formula: Wenennefer, meaning 'the one who continues to be perfect':

 *wnn-nfr*

Other phrases which appear in inscriptions

Dates

Although the Egyptians were quite aware of the exact length of the year and could have constructed a calendar if they wished, dates were instead recorded according to the regnal year – the number of years into – the reign of the current king or queen. The Egyptians used the decimal system, broken up into tens and units. The tens are indicated by repetition of the sign ∩ (so ∩ ∩ = 20) and the units by repetition of I (so III = 3). The dating formula has a fixed and regular form, and a typical formula might read:

rnpt-sp 16 ḫr ḥm nsw-bỉty Rꜥ-ms-s ꜥnḫ ḏr

The formula consists of the following components:

	*rnpt-sp*	regnal year		*ḥm*	person
	*ḫr*	under		*n*	of

From previous chapters, you will recognise the phrase 'King of Upper and Lower Egypt', and the name Ramses. The phrase at the end is an epithet, one of two commonly used at the end of a king's inscription:

 *ꜥnḫ ḏr* living enduringly

Thus the formula reads: 'Regnal year 16 under the person of the King of Upper and Lower Egypt, Ramses, living enduringly.' The alternate epithet reads:

 ^{c}*nḫ ḏt r nḥḥ* living enduringly and repeatedly

This sense of this phrase can be translated as 'for ever and ever'.

Other important phrases

It should also be mentioned here that royalty were not the only ones entitled to the title 'Osiris'. Deceased people of both sexes could also be addressed as 'Osiris', and their inscription often read 'the Osiris...' followed by their name. As noted in an earlier chapter, the Egyptians hoped to become one with this god after death, and this title demonstrates their belief that this unification had taken place.

Another important phrase is the abbreviation , which appears frequently on temple walls and elsewhere. It introduces words that are meant to be the speech of a god, and is to be read as *ḏd mdw,* meaning 'words spoken', or 'words to be spoken', and is usually followed by the phrase 'by god...' (or goddess), followed by the name of the god or goddess. The words which follow – which are somewhat ritualised, but too varied to be covered in this text – are the words spoken. This sign has a function similar to our quotation marks, in that it introduces direct speech.

Another expression that appears frequently on the outside of tombs is intended to be read aloud by passers-by, and is intended to provide a voice offering for the deceased. It was commonly used on the tombs of non-royal persons. Its initial phrase reads: 'O the living upon the earth who may pass this tomb':

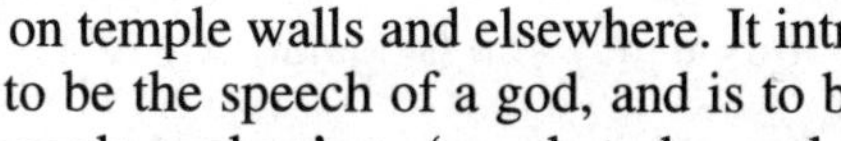

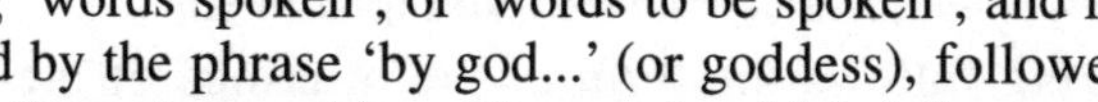

i	^{c}*nhw*	*tpw*	*t3*
O	the living	(who are) upon	the earth

The phrase 'who may pass by' is a form of the verb 'to pass' (by):

 *sw3ty.sn ḫr*

It is sometimes abbreviated  in this inscription. The complexities of this verb form are beyond the scope of this book, but in that it is often abbreviated anyway, read it as part of the whole inscription.

The final part is from the word 'tomb', to which the adjective 'this' has been added:

 *pn* this  *is pn* this tomb

The phrase that follows is a request from whoever 'passes by' to read the offering that the deceased has requested. It often takes the 'thousand of' form described in earlier paragraphs. The request is phrased 'may you say', followed by the voice offering:

 *ḏd=tn* may you (singular) say or

 *ḏd=tn* may you (plural) say

The offering follows the form of the offerings of the offering formula – a thousand of... and so on. These are phrases you already know from earlier.

SUMMARY

When you have completed the exercises in this chapter, look back on what you have achieved since starting this book. You are able to recognise many hieroglyphic signs – even if you still have to look some of them up, you are able to recognise a number of Egyptian words and phrases, and you are able to read major portions of inscriptions.

Is there more to learn? Sure there is.

Egyptian, as we said at the beginning, is as complex as any modern language, and able to express subtleties and nuances perhaps even better than most. Consider your learning in this book to be 'Phase 1' – or 'Egyptian 101' if you are an American!

So, what is in 'Egyptian 201'? Verb forms, in particular, are much more complex than can be covered here. Aside from funerary inscriptions, there are large numbers of narrative captions from the multitude of scenes of everyday life preserved in pictorial carvings. There are also narratives on tombstones that describe in some detail the life of the deceased. These require more complex verb forms and grammar than are detailed here. In the back of the book are listed some recommended books for self-study, and also the address of a modern day 'school for scribes'. But whatever your future course of study is beyond this book, you now have a solid grounding, and no small amount of knowledge to base additional study upon.

Exercises

Translate the following:

6.1 

6.2 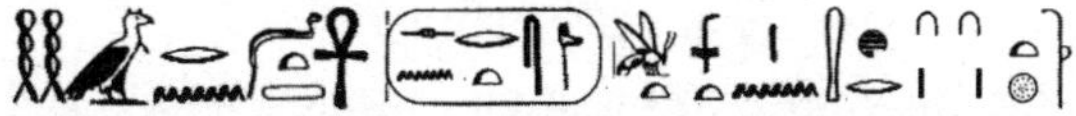

6.3 

7 MAYA HIEROGLYPHICS

Egypt and the Egyptians are familiar to most people; the Maya are much less so. Therefore this chapter concentrates in the main on the Maya as a people and as a culture, to give a background for the hieroglyphics that it is possible to cover herein. 'Possible', because Maya hieroglyphics are in the process of decipherment even as you read. Ironically, the decipherment of Maya hieroglyphics has been held back by exactly the same idea about them that retarded the decipherment of Egyptian hieroglyphics: that any given symbol stood for a complete word or concept. Egyptian hieroglyphics had to wait for a Campollion at the beginning of the nineteenth century; Maya decipherment has waited until only the last two decades to make the same start. The Egyptian model has been there all along, but the 'experts' refused to see it. Even more ironic is that the key has been there since the middle of the sixteenth century. Friar de Landa, the great persecutor of the Maya, wrote down a table of Maya symbols and the Spanish sounds they were equivalent to. Ignored for nearly four hundred years, it has, in fact been proven accurate.

Decipherment has progressed to the stage that several comparisons can be made between Egyptian and Maya writing. There are many principles with which you are already familiar:

1. Maya hieroglyphics are written as logograms – signs that stand for entire words, and phonograms – signs that stand for sounds within a word.
2. The Maya used determinatives – although in Mayan they were spoken as well as written.
3. Phonetic complements were frequently used.
4. Words were written in rectangular blocks as in

Egyptian. But in Mayan, the blocks were separated from each other to distinguish individual words.

Other methods of writing were different from Egyptian:

5 Mayan was read only from left to right and top to bottom.

6 The Maya used a form called a *semantic indicator* to tell you whether a sign was a logogram, phonogram, or determinative – sometimes.

7 The importance of metaphor can hardly be overemphasised: abstract ideas were uniformly expressed in this manner, thus great care must be taken by translators not to attach literal meanings to the associations. Metaphor could be used purely as an abstraction, or indicate a real bond with the metaphoric object. For example, the jaguar was a common metaphor for kingship, but there was also a bond between the king and actual jaguars: kings wore jaguar skins, sat on a carved-stone jaguar throne, and jaguars were sacrificed as part of kingly ritual. People are often referred to as maize or flowers – born to die, but carrying within themselves the seeds of regeneration. The water lily stood as a metaphor for the creation of earth – believed to have emerged from the primordial sea – and which seems to miraculously emerge from standing water.

8 And now for the really bad news: the Maya were never a unified culture like the Aztecs, and as a consequence, spoke a number of languages – some incomprehensible even to other Maya! The languages themselves were so convoluted and based on a culture so utterly foreign to our way of thinking that it is nearly impossible for someone who has not been brought up in that culture to understand them. But, there is also some good news.

9 As later paragraphs reveal, all of the Maya groups were preoccupied with time. Many of the surviving Mayan inscriptions and books – in whatever Mayan language – deal with calendars and genealogy. Most of the symbols relating to numbers and the calendars were universal across the Maya world; thus there is much repetition in the surviving glyphs, and learning to recognise a relatively few will allow you a certain access to Maya inscriptions. How all of this came about is part of the story of the Maya themselves, and is an important background to emphasis given to the hieroglyphs of this section of the book.

The Maya

The Egyptians were indisputably the premier ancient civilisation of the Old World, with a highly sophisticated language and writing. The only close parallel in the New World were the Maya, the most highly evolved – at least in some senses – of all ancient Mesoamerican cultures and, indeed, of most contemporary ancient civilisations, period. They possessed complex and intricately expressive written languages, an advanced mathematics, a calendar-system more advanced than our own, and a system of prediction and divination second to none. Their related astronomy was advanced enough to accurately predict celestial events like eclipses hundreds of years in advance. Their world-view echoes traditional eastern thought: the unity and interrelatedness of all things, both on the earth and beyond it.

Sometime in the last few centuries BC something happened to the Maya. Until that time they had been a scattered group of peoples living along the low-lying fringes of the Pacific Coast in what is now southern Mexico, Guatemala, and El Salvador. Other groups were in the same lowland fringes along the Caribbean in Honduras and Belize. Until that moment in history, they were still essentially a Stone Age people. Then, within a relatively short time, they acquired writing, mathematics, astronomy, and began to erect huge stone buildings in their jungle abode – a cultural upheaval similar to that of the Egyptians in 3100 BC.

It appears that the Maya acquired their new-found knowledge from the Olmecs, who lived much further north. The mystery surrounding the Olmecs is where they themselves came from, and indeed, who they even *were*. There is no evidence of an Olmec developmental phase anywhere in Mexico, or anywhere else in the New World, for that matter. It is clear that later cultures venerated the Olmecs, for in the much-later culture of the Aztecs, ancient Olmec ritual objects were collected and placed in positions of importance in their temples. Therefore much of Maya culture is part of an ancient culture much older than the Maya themselves, but which they brought, in many ways, to its highest form. Part of that culture was a system of writing every bit as complex and complete as that of the Egyptians. However, did Maya hieroglyphics come directly from the Egyptians? It is a question being debated by a number of modern writers and researchers, and the answer is: possibly.

Bearded White Men

Throughout the whole of the ancient world of Mexico and central America, are stories of 'bearded white men' who brought civilisation from 'the East'. There are variations on the basic story, but in most there is a leader often referred to as 'The Founder'. In central Mexico, stories about him were passed down through the Toltecs to the Aztecs, who called him *Quetzalcoatl*, meaning 'Plumed Serpent'. Carvings appear in even older Olmec contexts that clearly show bearded white men, predating the arrival of the Spanish in the 1500s by as much as two millennia.

Early stories of Quetzalcoatl collected in Mexico by Spanish chroniclers described him as 'a fair and ruddy-complexioned man with a long beard'. He was also said to be 'a white man; a large man, broad browed, with huge eyes, long hair, and a great, rounded beard'. He 'came from across the sea in a boat that moved by itself without paddles' – possibly meaning it had a sail. He 'built houses and showed couples that they could live together as husband and wife; and since people often quarrelled in those days, he taught them to live in peace.'[1] Further, Quetzalcoatl's symbol was the snake, leading to speculation that this was the Egyptian cobra, symbol of the Egyptian royal house, the spread hood of which might have appeared as a 'plume'.

[1] *North America of Antiquity*, p.286. Cited in: Ignatius Donelly, *Atlantis: The Antidiluvian World*, (New York: Harper Bros., 1882).

The ancient Mayan religious texts known as the *Books of Chilam Balam* report that the first inhabitants of Yucatan were the 'people of the serpent', who came from the east in boats with their leader, whose name means 'serpent of the east'. He was reputed to be a healer who could cure by laying on hands, and who revived the dead – a perfect description of the Egyptian god Horus, who was, among other things, the Egyptian god of healing.[2]

Itzamna, always represented as a wisened old man, is the oldest Mayan god, and who had many of the characteristics of Quetzalcoatl. It is likely that he is Quetzalcoatl in early Maya form. According to some Maya texts as many as twenty men came from the east in boats and stayed for ten years, described as wearing flowing robes, sandals, long beards and their heads were bare. Their leader was Itzamna, meaning 'Serpent of the east', a healer who could also cure by laying on hands, and who also revived the dead.[3] His companions were referred to as 'gods of fish', 'gods of agriculture', and a 'god of thunder' – 'Gods' in this case probably meant 'teachers'.

The great Maya book the *Popol Vuh* records the story of the heroic quest undertaken by three intrepid Maya nobles to the centre of all Mesoamerican civilisation, Tula. Three nobles 'journeyed to the east', and 'passed over the sea', to 'receive lordship'. The Lord of the East, whom the *Popol Vuh* calls Nacxit, was 'the great lord and sole judge over a populous domain'. During their stay they were 'given emblems of kingship' and were apparently educated, because they 'brought back the writing of Tulan, the writing of Zuyua [sounding similar to 'Libya', the ancient Egyptian name for 'Egypt'], and they spoke of their investiture in their signs and in their words'. Whether they actually went to Egypt or if they did indeed go to an Olmec Tula, the use of Egyptian-sounding names and Egyptian cultural symbols could easily have been part of the Olmec culture; for all we know, the Olmecs themselves may have been Egyptians, perhaps fleeing from the upheavals at the time of the collapse of the Old Kingdom when Egypt came under the yoke of the Hyskos in around 2400 BC – or perhaps even later, when the Persians conquered Egypt in the eighth century BC.

2 Peter Tompkins, *Mysteries of the Mexican Pyramids*, (London: Thames and Hudson, 1987), p.347.
3 Tompkins, p. 347.

There is other evidence that points to a possible Egyptian connection: the 'bearded white men' arrived in a boat made of snakes', a perfect description of a reed boat, with its undulations in the waves appearing as the writhing of snakes. Other evidence comes from the calendar: almost uniquely among ancient peoples, both the Egyptians and the Maya knew that the Earth's year is a bit over 365 days. While differing in the number of months, each have a basic 360-day calendar period plus five extra days. It wasn't until just a few centuries ago that we in the western world had a calendar as accurate. And, the earliest archaeological evidence for the Olmec civilisation starts about 2000 BC, yet the Olmecs and later the Maya used a calendar that began in 3114 BC – a date within a few decades of the founding of the Egyptian Old Kingdom.

While all of this could have been totally dismissed as pure speculation a few years ago, recent discoveries in Peru have cast a whole new light on the question of 'bearded white men'. Extensive ruins were discovered in the high mountains of northern Peru, in an area described by the Incas at the time of the Spanish conquest, to be the home of the 'Cloud People', described as 'beautiful people, tall, blue-eyed, blond and white-skinned'. In the vicinity of the Lake of the Condors. Nearby were cliff-tombs, unknown elsewhere in South America, in which we discovered the mummies of tall, white people, embalmed in a way never seen in South America before, but in a way similar to Egyptian mummies.

So, the question must inevitably arise as to whether Maya hieroglyphics are just later versions of Egyptian hieroglyphics, possibly brought to Mexico much earlier. On the face of it, it appears nonsense: there is no resemblance between the two. But that, too, is an appearance: while they are drawn with an entirely different set of symbols, the actual idea of them is identical – symbols that can stand for whole words, sounds, or ideas. And above all, there is the basic *idea* of writing itself, using familiar words as the basis for written sounds. This, as we saw in Chapter 1, was how Egyptian hieroglyphics apparently developed. It would be entirely natural and expected that once the idea was established, the Maya would use familiar *Mayan words and symbols* in their hieroglyphics.

Understanding The Maya World-View

Because language is ultimately about culture, there are some important aspects of Maya culture that underlie not only the words used in their languages, but in the structure of the languages themselves[4]. There are three pillars of Maya belief that are reflected in the majority of inscriptions: their beliefs about numbers, time, and the structure of the universe. It is around these that their languages are built, and it is from these that Maya hieroglyphics and their inscriptions can be interpreted.

Numbers

The whole of Maya life was built around numbers: numbers were believed to be sacred, and to have a life of their own. The Maya number-system was the best that existed anywhere in the world until the Arabs, centuries past the peak of Maya civilisation. With them, incredibly complex calculations allowed them to construct accurate tables for the prediction of eclipses, appearance of the Morning and Evening Star, mathematical tables, and to make predictions and prognostications that would dazzle a modern astrologer. Numbers form a large part of inscriptions and the surviving Maya books, thus they will be given emphasis here.

Time

Time was seen as circular and cyclical, with the events occurring in one cycle of time re-occurring in the next cycle. It was, surprisingly, a view of time not altogether different than that held by Einstein, or of modern eastern religions, represented by the Wheel of Karma. All of the Maya beliefs and ideas about time and numbers came together in the Maya calendar – or more properly, calendars. The *three* Maya calendars are about much more than time-keeping; they are a complex interweaving of a number of different cycles, all running at the same time. Each calendar cycle has its associated deities – and associated hieroglyphs – which both overlap and interpenetrate the various cycles. These glyphs make

4 The ancient Maya languages seem to have, at least in part, an ancestor of Cholon, in the same way that ancient Egyptian was an ancestor of Coptic.

up an important group of signs which appear in inscriptions, and they too will be covered.

Maya beliefs about time also generate some of the more difficult aspects of their language, and illustrate why it is difficult to translate, even where it is known. There is really nothing that we would recognise as past, present or future, either in Maya thinking or in Maya language and writing. A 'future' action is described – with varying verb forms and placement of nouns -according to the likelihood of its happening; an action taking place requires different forms depending on whether the action is completed or not, or whether it is just beginning or ending. There is a whole group of Maya signs used to differentiate time, movement, and action, called *aspect* words. Because time and space are interrelated, there is another group of descriptive words that place an object or person's position in space, all of which require different speech and written forms.

There is even more complexity than this, but it will serve to illustrate the focus of this book on easily translated glyphs which, fortunately, make up a considerable part of Maya inscriptions.

The Sky

The Maya were obsessed with the sky: major buildings in Maya cites not only had astronomical alignments themselves, they were also used for astronomical observations, with doorways and windows placed so that the movements of planets and other celestial objects could be observed and measured.

The Maya knew that the Morning and Evening Star were the same planet, almost uniquely in the ancient world. Highly accurate studies of Venus were made, tables of which form a considerable portion of the surviving Maya books. Venus fulfilled a similar role to that of Mars in the Old World – the symbol of war. In inscriptions the Venus glyph is often found above the glyph of a city attacked. The date for the attack was usually determined by the position of Venus.

Mars was also important, however its exact interpretation is still uncertain. It was studied almost as much as Venus, and accurate tables of the position of Mars, based on repetitions of the number

78 (Mars has a year of 780 days) form a portion of the Dresden Codex. Jupiter also appears to have symbolic and ritual associations, both with its full solar year of 12 Earth-years, and its half-cycle.

Figure 7.1 Glyphs for the earth and heavenly bodies

The Maya understood the universe to be a three-part structure: the Overworld, the Middleworld and the Underworld. The Overworld was the day sky, illuminated by the sun and the Underworld was the night sky which passed over humanity daily. The earth itself was believed to be flat; its surface upon which the Maya lived, was the Middleworld. The flat earth was said to be resting on the back of a monstrous crocodile. It was divided into 4 quarters, determined by the cardinal points of the compass. All three levels were joined with a central tree, its roots plunging into the Underworld, and its branches reaching up into the Overworld of the heavens. The central tree was green, with another four trees holding up the corners of sky at each cardinal direction. Each of the four trees had its own colour: red was the east and the rising sun; white the north, and the ancestral dead; yellow, the south, the right hand of the sun; and black, the west and the Underworld.

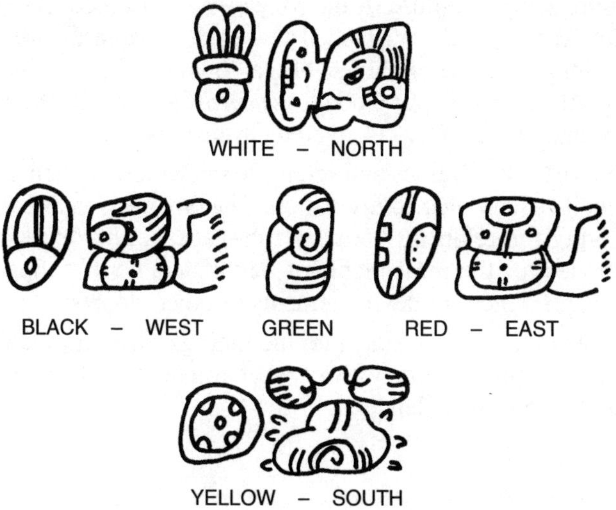

Figure 7.2 Glyphs for the world directions and their associated colours

The Overworld heavens are arranged in thirteen layers, with specific deities for each of them; the Underworld had nine such levels, each also with its god. The gods are in continuous interaction with each other, and are not separate from each other. The day- and month-glyphs in the following chapters are based on these and other gods, which are an integral part of the calendar system.

Surviving Maya books

When the Spanish arrived in the middle sixteenth century, they set about deliberately destroying the entire culture of Mexico and Central America. They quickly recognised that the writing of the Maya was central to both their culture and their belief system. The Spanish destroyed genealogies, biographies, collections of songs, and books on science, history, prophecy, astrology, and ritual. The first archbishop of Mexico boasted of destroying tens of thousands of books: in a single night in the Yucatan town of Mani, virtually the entire written culture of the Maya was consumed in one huge bonfire. Thanks to the misplaced zeal of the Spaniards, we are left with only four remaining Maya books written in Maya hieroglyphics: the Paris Codex, the Dresden Codex, the Madrid Codex, and the recently discovered Grolier Codex.

All four discuss religious and scientific matters, with their contents principally given over to divination. The emphasis is astrological, specifying the relations between time, space, and deities, along with tables for the movements of Venus, a table of eclipses, and possible references to the movements of other planets.

In the next chapter, we start into the hieroglyphs that relate to the coming together of many threads of Maya thought and belief: Maya numbers and calendars.

8 MAYA NUMBERS AND CALENDARS

Numbers

It is no exaggeration to say that the whole of Maya life was built around numbers, believed to be sacred, and to virtually have a life of their own. The majority of surviving Maya inscriptions have numbers somewhere within them (see Chapter 7). Exactly how sacred numbers were is demonstrated in the alternate set of symbols used from time to time in important inscriptions: each number has a hieroglyphic equivalent, all of which are images of gods, which can be the face of the god, or a full figure. In the earliest inscriptions the deity is a full figure, carrying the number or unit on his back.

Within their highly sophisticated and useable number-system they possessed two rarities in ancient history – the zero and the number place-system. Thus a number-place could be 'empty' – a zero – as '1s' place is when we reach 10 in the 10-based system. For the first time in the New World, and far ahead of any of their contemporaries in the Old World, numbers could be manipulated easily, and complex calculations such as the prediction of eclipses and planetary movements became possible. Their application of numbers to the passage of time created a mathematical divination similar to modern astrology – although much more complex!

The Maya number-system was vigesimal, that is, based on divisions of 20: presumably in a climate where people went barefoot, it was just as easy to continue counting on the toes as well as the fingers! In the elegant and sophisticated number system of the Maya, only three symbols were needed to write any number: a dot for '1'; a bar, for '5', and a seashell for '0'. So in the '1s' column in our system, when we reach 10 the zero appears. But in the Maya system, this happens when we reach 20.

As numbers get larger, the number of 'places' expands to accommodate them as in our system, except the places are based on 20 rather than 10 as in our system. The next place in the 10-based system is 100 – ten 10s – but in the Maya system this does not happen until there are twenty 20s – in other words, 400. Likewise in the 10-based system, the next place, the thousands, appears when we accumulate ten 100s. In the Maya system it happens when we accumulate twenty 400s, or 8,000. As we are used to the 10-based system, at first glance the Maya system seems unwieldy, but in fact, it allows exactly the same complex calculations – along with the ability to express very large numbers – as the 10-based system. Maya numbers are read vertically, with the lowest values, the '1s' column, at the bottom. They can also be written horizontally, with the number places larger the further to the left that they extend – exactly as our number places do.

Let's take a look at the structure of Maya numbers:

For numbers below 19 there is just a simple combination of bars and dots:

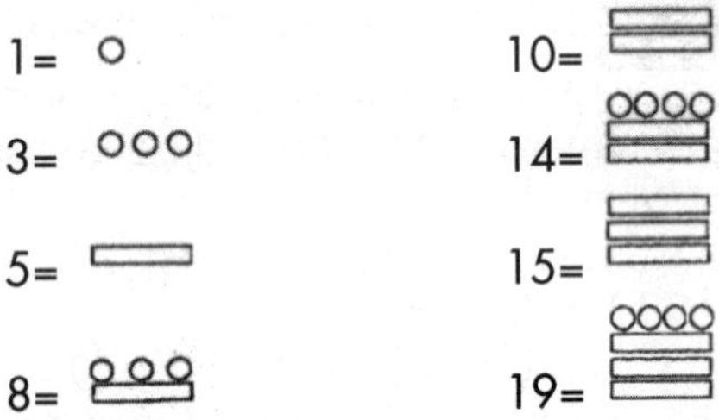

When the first '20s' place is filled, the dot for 1 twenty moves into the next higher place (as the '1' does in the 10-based system), and the 0 fills the empty '1s' place:

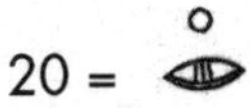

For numbers between 21 and 40, the '10s' place fills exactly as in the example above:

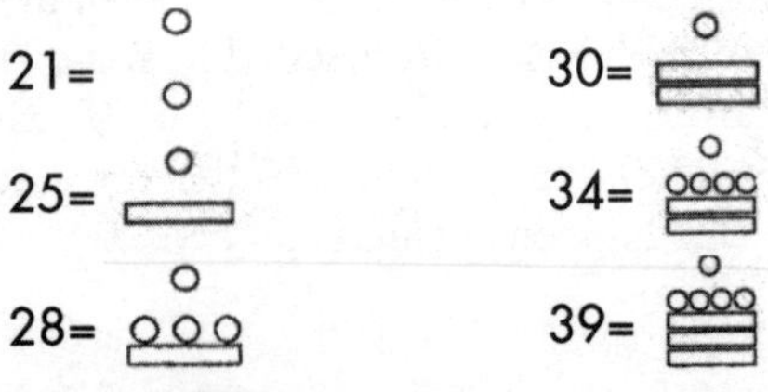

When the second '20s' place is filled, two dots appear in the '20s' column:

40= 

This same pattern repeats until the '20s' place itself reaches 20, when a new columns appears, the '400s' column:

20 x 20 = 400 = 

Exercise

Here are some of the numbers between 40 and 400. See if you can interpret them:

8.1 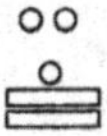

8.2 

8.3 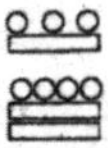

8.4 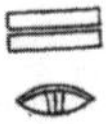

8.5 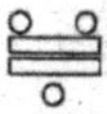

8.6 

8.7 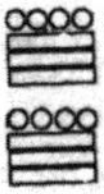

The next number-place in the Maya system was 20 × 400, or 8000, noted in exactly the same way as the previous places:

8000 = 

And so on for as many places as necessary, each new place being 20 times the previous. There is quite literally no limit to the size of the numbers that can be written in Maya notation.

As mentioned earlier, Maya numbers can also be written horizontally, for example:

2 =  7 =  17 =  29 =  and so on.

There is one additional sign of note when reading Maya numbers. In fact, it is not really a 'sign' at all, in that it is not read, but rather it serves as a 'space filler' to artistically balance the number glyph. It takes the form of a rounded crescent, and is usually used to fill in the space between the dots when a two or three appears as part of the number-glyph:

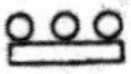

The sacred nature of Maya numbers is illustrated by the fact that they can also be 'written' using the heads of gods as number symbols. These are shown in Figure 8.1, with their spoken equivalent in Yucatec, a current language of the northern Maya.

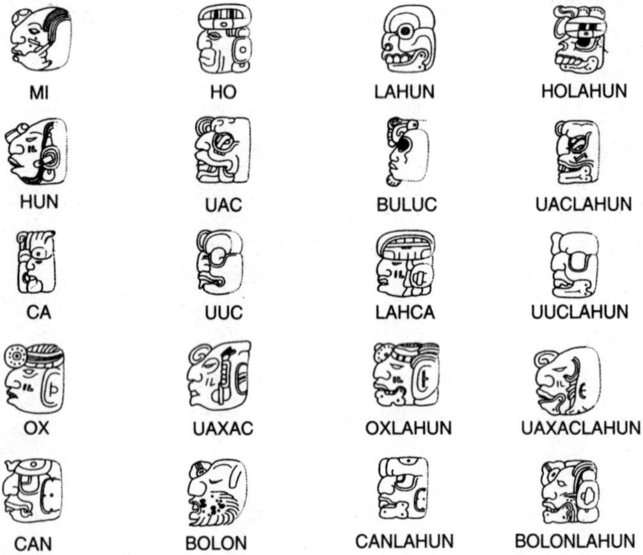

Figure 8.1 Number equivalents as heads of gods

With the flexibility of Maya numbers, incredibly complex calculations allowed the construction of highly accurate tables for the prediction of eclipses, planetary movements, the appearance of the Morning and Evening Star, mathematical tables, and to make predictions and prognostications of stunning complexity. It was all written down in books for many years in advance, or more accurately, as many *days* in advance because all Maya astronomical calculations were calculated in numbers of days, and not on calendar dates.

Calendars

Far from being simple time-keepers, the Maya calendars are a complex interweaving of several different cycles, all running at the same time. Each calendar cycle has its associated deities, which both overlap and penetrate. The various cycles of the calendar also overlap the four quarters of the universe and interconnect with each of the cycles. The 'daykeepers', those who kept track (and still keep track) of all the various cycles and calendars, were not only very busy, but highly skilled mathematicians as well!

The Sacred Calendar

The Sacred Calendar of the Maya is also referred to as the *Ritual Almanac*. It is a cycle of 260 days, and it was and still is, mainly used for religious purposes, divination and acting as the chief guide to ceremonial activity. It in turn is composed of two smaller

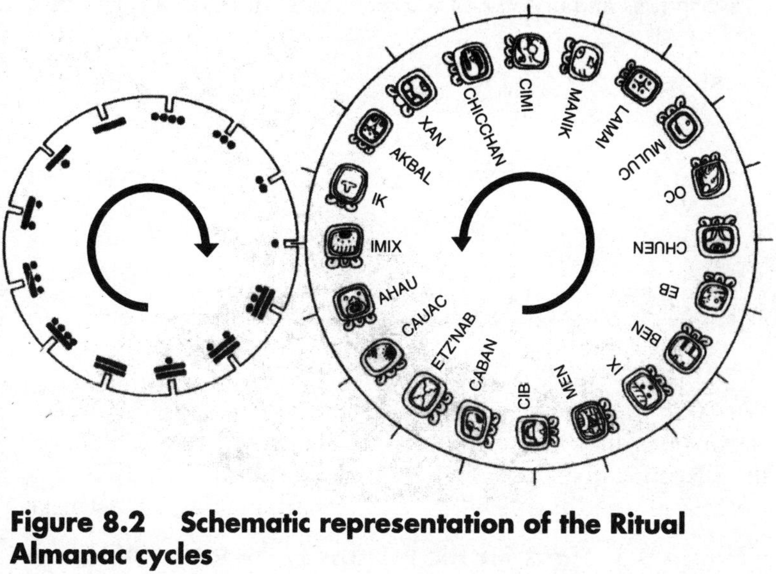

Figure 8.2 Schematic representation of the Ritual Almanac cycles

interlocking cycles, one comprising 20 days, each with its own overseeing god, and the other of 13 numbers. The cycles can be most easily imagined as two intermeshing gears, one with 13 teeth, and the larger with twenty. A number of theories have been put forth for the significance of the 260 day cycle, the most likely of which is that it is close to length of the human gestation period.

Each of the 20 days is designated by both a number and a name. For example, at the start of the 260-day cycle when the days and numbers are synchronised, the first day is Imix, so the first day of the cycle is designated 1 – Imix. The second day of the cycle is named Ik, and is called 2 – Ik. The 13th day of the cycle is Ben, and is therefore 13 – Ben. But, the 14th day of the cycle, Ix, has used up all of the 13 numbers, so the number cycle begins again. Thus it is called 1 – Ix. And so on recycling each of the 13 numbers through the remaining 20 days. But when the 20 days are completed and the 20 day cycle begins again with Imix, only 7 of the 13 numbers have been used up, thus the designation of the 21st day of the cycle is 8 – Imix, the 22nd day 9 – Ik, and so on. The next time 1 – Imix appears will be on the 261st day, thus completing the 260 day cycle.

The glyphs for the days of the Ritual Almanac appear in inscriptions and in some of the remaining Maya books. They are:

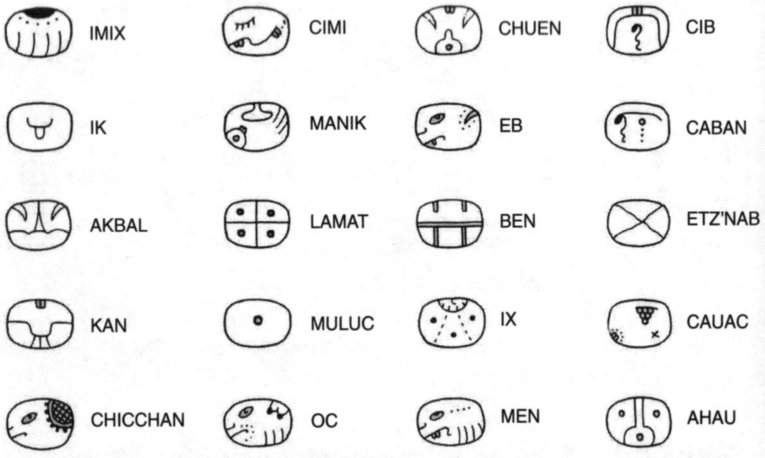

Figure 8.3 Signs for the months in the Ritual Almanac

The Solar Calendar

The solar calendar corresponds closely to the 365 $^1/_4$ day solar year, and is comprised of 18 months of 20 days each, along with an additional five day period to make up the total of 365 days. The Maya knew that the actual year was $^1/_4$ of a day longer, but they apparently saw no need for a leap-year, thus this calendar is generally referred to as the Vague Year. Each month is named for a god, and each of the days are designated by a number, as with our own calendar. The first day of the month is the '0' day, referred to as the 'seating' day. It is the day in which the month-god settles into his new routine for that month. According to Maya philosophy, the influence of any particular time span starts before the actual span numerically begins, and persists beyond the time of its numerical ending. For example, the first month of the Maya Vague-Year calendar is named after Pop, so the first day of Pop – written 0-Pop – is actually transcribed as 'the seating of Pop'. Thus the twentieth day of the month of Pop is actually designated 19-Pop, followed on the succeeding by the seating day of the next month-god Uo – 0-Uo. And again this follows through for twenty days until 19-Uo, the day after which becomes the seating of the next month-god Zip, and so on through the year. At the 360th day – 19-Cumku – comes the five day period called Uayeb, days considered particularly unlucky.

Because the cycles of the *Ritual Almanac* and the *Vague Year* run concurrently, any given day will normally have two identifications: its *Vague Year* designation and its *Ritual Almanac* designation. The start of the two calendars corresponds only every fifty-two years, called the Calendar Round, a particularly sacred period of time to the Maya. It was seen as a time of the dying out of the old and the rebirth of the new. At the end of each Calendar Round cycle, pyramids were re-faced with stone, adding another layer, and also giving us a way of dating the age of the pyramids – like counting the rings in a tree. Houses were pulled down and rebuilt, and there was a general refurbishment of the entire material culture.

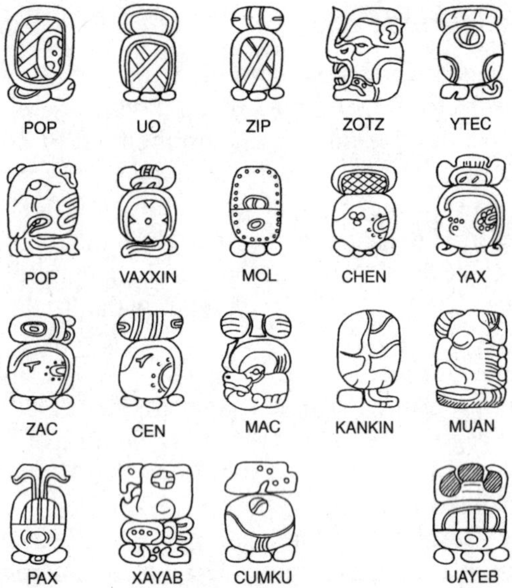

Figure 8.4 Glyphs for the months of the Vague Year

The Long Count Calendar

Because every Calendar Round cycle is identical to the last and repeats every 52 years, the question when examining dates across the whole of Maya history, is *which* 52-year period. The Maya had the same question, which was answered by the third calendar, the *Long Count Calendar*. This calendar began on the 13th of August, 3114 BC and, as with our own calendar, it was not used just for keeping track of days – for predicting which days will fall in what position – but also in keeping track of past events, relationships between those events in terms of their time occurrence, and for understanding the patterns of those events. Long Count dates were also used to establish the long-term lineages of the ruling classes, and to position the *Ritual Almanac* and the *Vague Year* cycles, which were more for 'everyday' use. The Long Count is actually a count of days and is written as an accumulation of various time periods, calculated in days. It is a principal feature of nearly every Maya inscription for most of Maya history. Its use only disappeared after the conquest of the Maya by the Toltecs in 983 AD, when the lineage of rulers no longer became an issue. The Toltec rulers knew exactly who they were!

The Long Count Calendar is based on a 360 day period called a *tun*. The *tun* is comprised of 18 *Unials* of 20 days each, each day being called a *kin*. 20 *tuns* make up a *katun* of 7,200 days, and 18 *katuns* are a *baktun* of 144,000 days. There are 13 *baktuns* in a Great Cycle. According to Maya belief, at the end of each Great Cycle, also called a 'Sun', a great catastrophe overtakes the planet, most of humanity is wiped out, and civilisation must start again. We are believed to be in the Fifth Sun, which comes to an end on December 23, 2012. It is the basis of what is commonly referred to as the Maya Prophecy. 'Prophecy' is really a misnomer, because it implies revelation from a divine source – the Maya Prophecy is nothing more than the end of a Maya Great Cycle. Will anything actually happen on that date? We don't have long to wait to find out!

1 kin	=		1 Day
20 kins	=	Unial	20 days
18 unials	=	Tun	360 days
20 tuns	=	Katun	7,200 days = 20/360-day years or about 19.7/365.25-day (solar) years
20 katuns	=	Baktun	144,000 days = 400 / 360-day years or about 394/365.25-day (solar) years

Two types of glyphs were used to designate the time periods of the Long Count, depending on whether it was written (painted) or carved:

Figure 8.5 Variations of the Long Count Glyphs used in inscriptions

The oldest monument dated in the Long Count so far discovered is a stela at Chiapa de Corzo, a major ceremonial centre, a date corresponding to the 7th of December, 36 BC.

Long Count dates are usually written in one of two ways: as a single vertical column (see Figure 8.6) with the baktun number at the top and working downwards, or as a double column with the baktun number to the right of the Introducing Glyph, and then moving in succession through double columns (see Figure 8.7)[1]. Other components of the date-block will often be the current Vague Year date, and/ or the current Ritual Almanac date. Also included are likely to be information about the phase and lunation (full-moon cycle) the date embraces, as in the figure.

Figure 8.6 Full initial series Long Count Date

[1] Drawn from Henderson, 1998, p. 118.

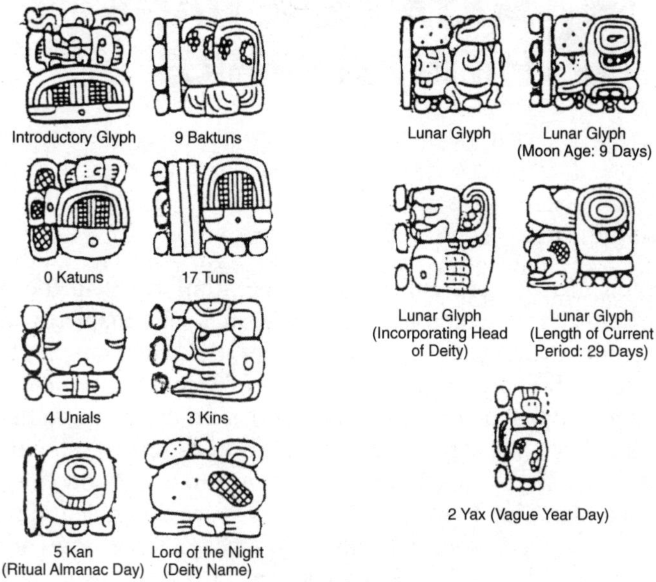

Figure 8.7 Full Initial Series Long Count Date

Exercise

Translate the following dates*:

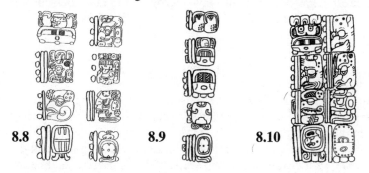

8.8 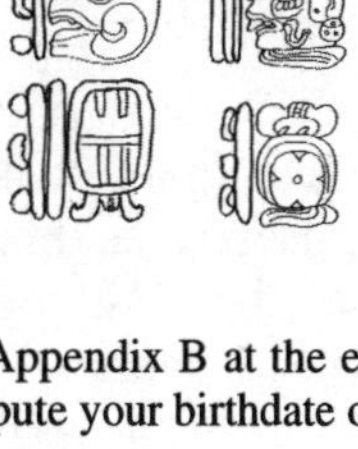

8.9 

8.10 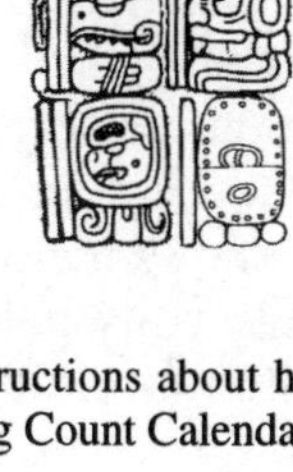

*In Appendix B at the end of the book, you will find instructions about how to compute your birthdate or other important dates in the Long Count Calendar.

9 MAYA LANGUAGE HIEROGLYPHICS

As noted in Chapter 7, there are some similarities in the way Mayan and Egyptian hieroglyphics are written; this chapter focuses more on the differences. As noted earlier, the Maya languages of the hieroglyphics are infinitely more complex and convoluted than Egyptian, and those portions presented herein are no more than a 'taster', in hope that some readers will follow further developments as new strides are taken in translation; and, beyond that, in understanding. Simply reading the words is one thing; determining their meaning is another thing altogether. As we saw in the Egyptian section, language always is a reflection of the culture within which it develops, and the language of the Maya – apart from the physical remains of their ancient culture – remains the greatest source of information about it. Thus unravelling Maya hieroglyphics is about revealing the Maya themselves.

There are a few points about Maya hieroglyphics that can be useful learned here. Their physical appearance is a good place to begin, and is one point of difference from the Egyptian.

The Maya Phonetic Alphabet

This table of sounds corresponds roughly to the bilaterals of Egyptian – the dual-consonant sounds. However, the Maya *did* write out vowel sounds, and the table records the known versions of the consonant-vowel sounds thus far known. The first row of the table shows the signs for the vowel-sounds themselves, and below are the consonant-vowel signs. For example, the signs of the second line are the signs for the ba, be, bi, and bu sounds. As is instantly apparent, there are more than one sign for most of the sounds. The why? of this is hard to answer: it may be that the use of a particular sign was entirely based on the artistic whim of the carver or painter; it may be that several signs evolved over time, and there were cultural reasons for using a particular sign at a particular place; it may be that there are dimensions or slight variations in pronunciation that are yet unknown. Whatever the answer may be, the use of multiple signs complicates the task of the translator.

Table 9.1

	a	e	i	o	u

b					
ch					
ch′					
h					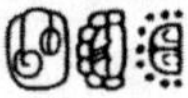
c					
k					
l					
m					

Table 9.1 – continued

	a	e	i	o	u
n					
p					
s					
t					
tz					
dz					
u					
x					
y					

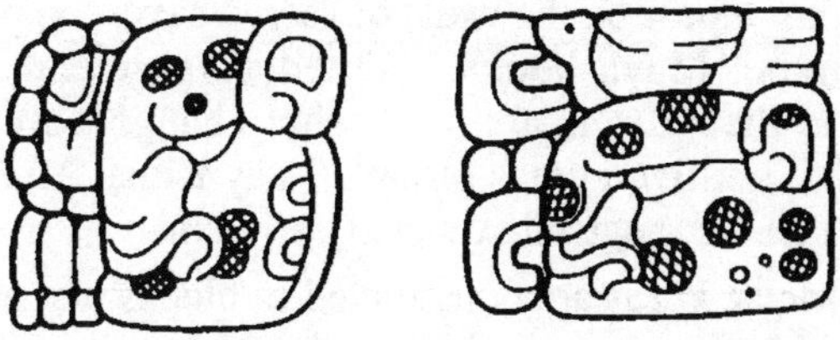

Figure 9.1 Variations on the 'jaguar' glyph

The next major difference is that the signs are not always carved or painted uniformly. In Egyptian, we saw that all that varied was the size; in Mayan, the actual glyph may vary widely. For example, in the figure above we see the glyphs for the names of two Maya rulers: Shield-Jaguar and Bird-Jaguar. Note that the 'jaguar' portion of the glyph, while still retaining their basic elements, are drawn in very different proportions from each other.

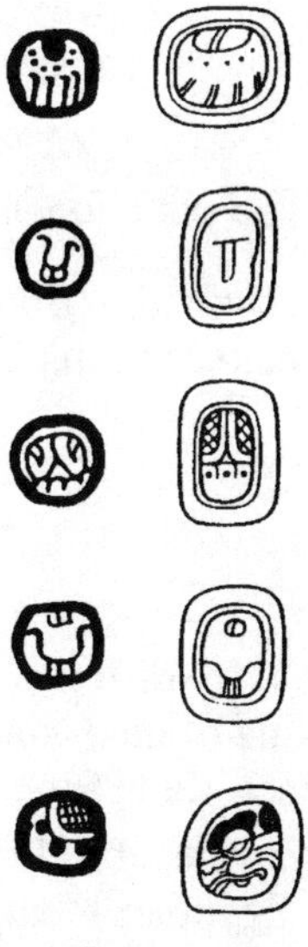

Figure 9.2 Variations between painted and carved forms

There is also a difference between painted and carved glyphs. Painted glyphs appear on the walls of sacred caves, on pottery, and in the surviving Maya books. Painted glyphs tend to be less detailed, and their forms are somewhat changed. In the figure above are the first five glyphs of the 20-day Ritual Almanac cycle which illustrate the range of expected variations.

In general, Maya words are constructed in blocks just as Egyptian words; but in Maya hieroglyphics each word is a separate block, and the individual components of the word are merged into a single picture – a sort of 'joined up' writing. The 'jaguar' glyph – the Maya word *balam* – also demonstrates the various ways it was possible for a scribe to write any given word:

First, it can be written purely as a logogram, as in Egyptian:

Second, it can be written as a logogram with phonetic compliments (also as in Egyptian):

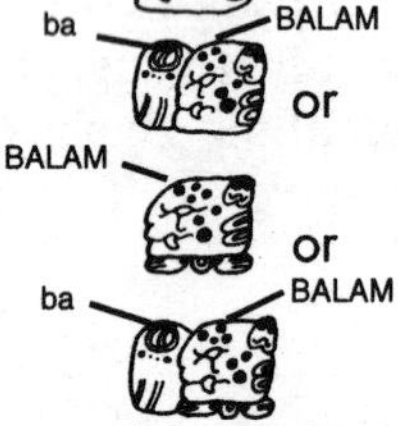

And finally, it can be spelled out phonetically:

Another situation occurs when the final vowel sound is not pronounced, as in the word *dzib*, 'writing':

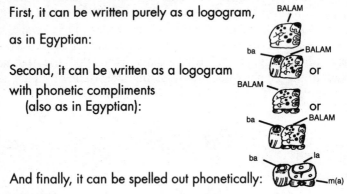

It is possible that this implies two different types of writing, but no evidence has been forthcoming of this. Note also that the *dzi* glyph has been turned horizontal (see Table 9.1).

In creating a word, the components of its block are often rearranged for aesthetics – again as in Egyptian – but often the relative sizes and shapes are changed as well, as described above. The name of a famous warrior captain of the Itzas, Kakupacal, appears in a number of places at the major city of Chichen Itza, in several forms. Here are two of them[1]:

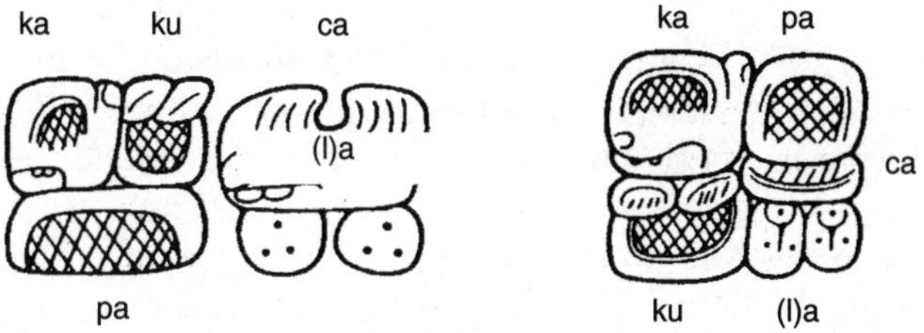

Figure 9.3 Variant spellings of Kakupacal

Aside from changing size and form somewhat, sometimes the glyphs are even merged, a term called *conflation*. Here is an example, the words *chum tun*, the 'seating of the tun'[2]:

Figure 9.4 Conflation of *chum tun*. All four examples spell *chum tun*

There are several glyphs that appear in Maya inscriptions that are worth memorising. Because inscriptions dealt in the main with dynastic matters of the ruler there are, as in Egyptian, certain notations that are to be expected: the date of the ruler's birth and accession in *Long Count*, *Ritual Almanac*, and *Vague Year* dates, as in Chapter 8; the date on which the ruler came to power; the name and titles of the ruler; and, his age in katuns at the time of his accession. There may also be a notation of which ruler he is within his line, the 'succession' glyph. Let's look at the glyphs for each of these notations:

[1]After Kelly, 1976.
[2]After Coe, 1992.

The untranslated Birth Glyph, the so-called 'upended frog' glyph, preceding the date glyphs for the ruler's birth dates.

The as yet untranslated Accession Glyph, the so-called 'toothache' glyph, preceding the accession date glyphs.

Ti Kal Copán Palenque

The ruler's names and titles, which often include the city-name of his rulership. Shown are the glyphs for three of the major cities.

a b

The *ahau-katuns* glyph, the ruler's age in katuns at the time of accession, *a* indicates the 2nd katun, *b* the 4th katun. *Ahau* means 'lord'.

Although rulers were all men, important women also featured in inscriptions. The glyph shown preceded female names and titles.

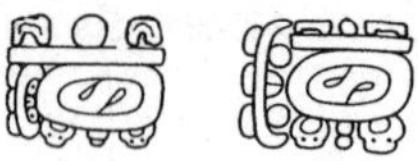

The 'change of office' glyph, of uncertain translation. This glyph shows where the new ruler is within the line of succession. Shown are two versions of the 6th in succession.

Also within the notations of succession may be included glyphs relating to the relationship of the new ruler to others.

u nichin
'child of' (father)

yal
'child of' (mother)

sucu uinic
'elder brother'

There is one more glyph that appears in inscriptions and captions: the 'captive' glyph. The Maya cities were frequently at war with each other, for the most part as a source of captives for sacrifice. Royal captives were especially prized, and their capture was often celebrated in a mural or inscription. As with other inscriptions, dates are a major portion, along with the names of the captors and captives. the glyph which accompanies the captives name is:

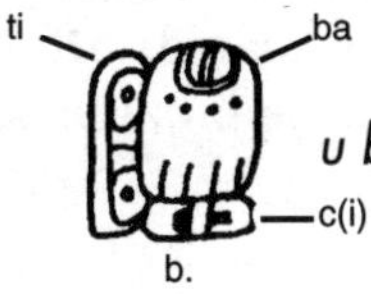

u bac 'his captive'

Just for Fun

To conclude the section on Maya hieroglyphics on a somewhat lighter note, you can use the phonetic signs table at the beginning of the chapter to construct English names in Maya signs.

1 First, sound out the name in consonant-vowel segments. If a consonant-vowel segment is not possible, use the following formula: where the consonant has a hard pronunciation, use the consonant-vowel combination with an *a* ending: John = *Ja n*(*a*)

When it has a soft sound, use an *i* ending: Jane = *Ja n*(*i*)

2 Second, choose the symbols from the table. There is an immediate problem with both of these names: a lack of a *J* sound. When a sound-sign is lacking, choose the nearest to it. In this case the *ch'* sign has been chosen. This is a glottal, and thus is closer to the English sound than the *ch* sound. Thus we have *ch'a n*(*a*) and *ch'a n*(*i*). For the ending syllable, choose a glyph that is a full-round glyph, when you have the option:

ch'a n(a) John

ch'a n(i) Jane

Remember that transliterating one language into another is always an approximation, and you have to do the best you can. Notably absent from the table is an *r* sound. Depending on the pronunciation, the *l* sound is an approximation. Thus Mary becomes *Ma li*:

Ma li Mary

Or, it may be omitted altogether if it makes the pronunciation even further away: Martha becomes Ma ta, and Peter becomes Pi ta:

Ma ta Martha

Pi ta Peter

You will see that there are alternative glyphs for many of those above. They are all correct – depending on your artistic inclinations!

Conclusion

Although the Maya section is much more abbreviated than the Egyptian section, it is hoped that it will encourage readers to look further. New websites are appearing almost weekly as further strides are made in translation, refer to the Further Reading section (p.000) for books that will also add to your knowledge. Without a doubt Maya is much harder than Egyptian, but even with the signs and symbols revealed in this book, you can make a start on opening the door into their remarkable culture.

APPENDIX A

Table of Egyptian hieroglyphic signs

Full-figure human signs

 seated man d=man, occupations of men, 'I', 'me', or 'my'

 seated woman d=woman, occupations of women

 goddess with feather *m3*^{c}*t,* harmony

 seated god d=names of gods, titles of gods

 seated man, hand to mouth d=eat, speak, emotion

 man striking with stick d=effort, action, violence

 official holding flail *špsy*, dignified

 man leaning on stick *í3w*, old

 man leaning on forked stick *smsw*, elder, eldest

 official with staff *sr*, official (as in 'an official')

 kneeling in adoration *hnw*, jubiliation

 soldier *mš*^{c}, soldier or military expedition

 infant *ẖrd*, child

 slumped man d=tired, weak

 man with arms raised d=adoration

 man with arms raised d=joy, rejoice

 man standing, hand to mouth *srḫ*, to talk about or accuse

man gesturing *ỉ*, the interjection 'O'

fallen man with blood d=enemy

man falling d=fall, fell, overthrow

man building a wall d=build (also an abbreviation for *ikd* builder)

man striking *ḥwỉ*, strike

mummy on bier, death, or lying down

priest pouring libation *wꜥb*, priest

figure of Amun *ỉmn*, the god Amun

royal figure *nsw*, king + attached to names for the god Osiris

royal figure with flail, variant of

man with dagger *ỉry*, d=keeper

man with basket d=work

bound man d=captive

Signs representing parts of the human body

eye *ỉr*, do or make

hair d=hair

head in profile *tp*

face *ḥr*, upon, on account of

raised arms *k3*, immortal soul

arms showing denial *n* or *nn* added to words to form negatives

arms with shield and ax *ꜥḥ3*, fight

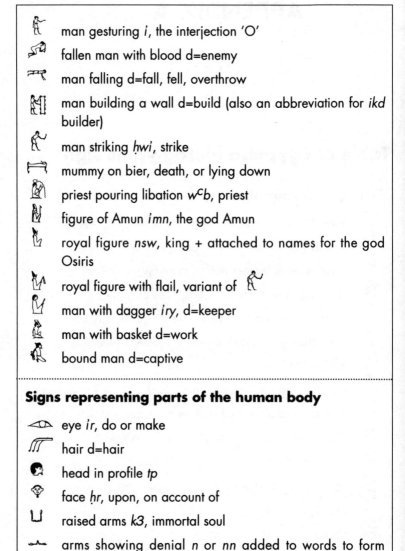

arm holding wand *ḏsr*, sacred

arm with flail *ḫw*

arm holding stick d=effort, action, violence

arm offering loaf *di͗* or *rdi͗*, give

lower arm ^{c}

hand *d*

mouth *r* at, towards people

water jug on 'motion' sign *i͗n(i͗)*, bring

legs walking forward d=forward, *iw(i)*, come, *nmtt*, journey

legs walking backward d=return, (to go) back, run

water pouring from jug *w^{c}b*, jug rests atop leg, symbol for *b*

leg *b*

breast d=breast or suckle

penis *mt*, male

arms embracing *ḥm*, sign *ḥm-k3*, ka priest away

toes? *s3h*

god with year sign *Ḥh*, the god Heb, *ḥh* million

Signs featuring birds or parts of birds

falcon with human head *r^{c}*, (the god) Re

Hw.t-Hr Hathor (lit: the mansion of Horus)

falcon falcon, *ḥr*, (the god) Horus

sacred ibis *ḏḥwty*, the god Thoth

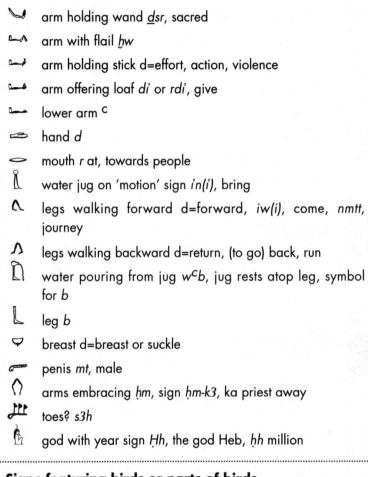

 egg *3st*, the goddess Isis

 human-headed bird *b3*, soul

 duckling *ṯ3*

 duck's head *3pd*, bird

 trussed goose d=goose (species of)

 flying duck *p3*

 goose *gb*, bird

 pintail duck *s3*, bird

 guinea fowl *nḥ*

 buzzard *tw*

 vulture *3*

 owl *m*, in, from, as, with

 quail chick *w*

 black ibis *gm*

 vulture *mt*

 swallow *wr*

 sparrow d=small, weak, pathetic

 jabiru *b3*

 cormorant *ʿk*

 feather *šw*

 crested ibis *3ḫ*

 heron *bnw*

Signs based on mammals or parts of mammals

 dog on shrine *ỉnpw*, the god Anubis

 dog on standards *wp-w3wt*, the god Wepwawet

 animal-headed god *sty*, the god Seth

 piece of flesh *3st*, another ideogram for Isis

 newborn calf *ỉw*

 head of ox *k3*, ox

 ox d=ox, bull, cattle (species of)

 ox tongue *ns*

 ox ear *sḏm*, hear

 ox horns *wp*

 rabbit or hare *wn*

 desert dog d=dog (species of)

 head of dog *wsr*

 three fox pelts *ms*

 lion's hindquarter *ph*

 lion *rw*

 front of lion *ḥ3t*, front, d=front

 spine with marrow *rw*

 spine with marrow *ỉm3ḫ*, veneration

 heart *ỉb*, heart

 animal belly *ẖ*

 goat hide *ẖn*

 heart and windpipe *nfr*, beauty, be beautiful

 pustule d=disease, scent, odour

 placenta? *ḫ*

Signs based on fish, reptiles and insects

 mummified crocodile *3bk*, the god Sobek

 cobra *ḏ*

 pair of crocodiles *ỉty*, sovereign

 fish *ẖ3*

 horned viper *f*

 dung beetle *ḫpr*, become, happen

 bee *bỉty*, king

Signs from the sky

 sun disc r^{c}, the sun, day, time, The god Re or Ra

 sun with rays, light

 sunrise *ḫc*

 star and crescent *3bd*, month

 star d=*star* (name of), *dw3*, adore, *wnwt*, priesthood

 crescent moon d=moon or lunar-based event, or *ỉcḥ*, moon

 the arch of the sky d=sky, *ḥry*, that which is upon

Signs from the landscape

 valley *ḏw*

 slope *k*

 strip of land *t3*, or *ḏr*, eternity

 alternative for above

- sand dunes *h3st*, foreign land d=desert (name of)
- grains of sane d=mineral (name of)
- rippled water *mw*, d=body of water (name of)
- water *n*, for, towards a place
- well with water *ḥ*
- pool with flowers *š3*
- pool *š*
- pattern of irrigation canals *sp3t*, district
- irrigation canals, irrigated land
- road boardered by shrubs *w3t*, road

Signs from plants

- papyrus plants *ḥ3*
- lorus plant *ẖ3*
- herbs *ḥn* d=plant (name of)
- double-reed leaf *ỉ* or *y*
- reed leaf *ỉ* or *y*
- cluster of reeds *sẖt*, countryside d=countryside (name of area)
- bundle of reeds *ỉs*
- thorn, sharp or keen
- crossed sticks, separate, pass by
- twisted flax wick *h.*
- bundle of flax *ḏr*
- tree d=tree, *ỉ3m*, *ỉm3*
- notched palm *mp*, year

tree branch *ẖt*

stick *mdw*, stick, language, words spoken

walking stick, variation of

log with bark removed d=scent or scented wood

pair of rushes *nn*

flowering sedge *3m*^{c}, 'Upper Egypt'

sedge plant *sw*, *nsw*, king

grape arbour d=vineyard

scented pod or rhysome d=sweet (name of)

scented pod or rhysome alternative for

Signs based on tools or weapons

crook *ḥḳ3*, *ḥḳ3*, ruler

crook with binding *šms*, follow

pestle *ti*

fire drill *ḏ3*

drill drilling bead *wb3*

chisel *3b* or *mr*

scribe's implements *sẖ*, scribe

fuller's club *hm*

sickle *m3*

adze *stp*, select or choose

plough *šn*^{c}, *hb*, d=plough

hoe *mr*

lasso *w3*

twisted cord *šs*

twisted cord *šn*

coil of rope w

cattle hobble *mḏw*, ten

tether rope *ṯ*

whip? *mḥ*

arrowhead *sn*

mace *hḏ*

harpoon w^{c}

throwing stick *bḥ* or *ḥw*

sledge *tm*

Signs based on religious symbols

combined signs *nbt-ḥwt*, the goddess Nephthys

carrying chair *3sir*, the god Osiris

seat *st*, place or seat, *3s(t)* in the god Osiris, and *3st* the goddess Isis

totem? *mnw*, the god Min

shrine *sḥ*, shrine

standard with feather *i̓mnt*, the west

pennant *nṯr*, god (note inclusion of *nṯr* in next symbol)

cemetery *ẖrt-nṯr*, cemetery ('place of the gods')

alternative for

papyrus roll d=abstractions, write

sceptre *ḫrp*, control

Signs connected to buildings

palace facade ^{c}*ḥ*, palace

house plan *pr*, house

courtyard *h*

plan of estate *hwt*, enclosure, foundation

roads within walls *nwt*, town d=town

pillar *ỉwn*, pillar, *ỉwnw*, Heliopolis

wooden column ^{c}*3*

wooden column ^{c}*3*

reed column *ḏd*

lid or door d=open

door bolt *sz*

threshing floor *sp*

grain measure *s˘nwt*, granary

Signs based on containers or household items

pot *ỉn* or *nw*

beer jug *ḥnḳt*, beer

bowl *3bt*

basket *nb*

basket *k*

ointment jar d=ointment (name of)

water pot with water flow *ḳbḥw*, libation water and related words

rack of water pots *ḫnt*, in front of, foremost

 alternative for 

 milk jug in net *mỉ*

 water skin *šd*

 jar stand *g*

 basin with canopy *ḥb*, festival, d=festival

 alabaster bowl, alterntive for 

 wicker stool *p*

 plinth $m3^{c}$

 gaming board *mn*

Signs connected to food

 offering loaf *dỉ* or *rdỉ*, give

 bread loaf *t*

 small loaf *t*, bread

 bread loaf on mat *ḥtp*, offer

 offering load d=bread, offerings

Signs connected to boats

 sail *t3w*, breath

 oar *ḫrw*, voice

 boat with furled sail, to sail downstream

 boat with full sail, to sail upstream

Signs based on clothing or ornaments

 sandal strap *cnḫ*, life

 folded cloth *s*

 fringed cloth *mnḫt*, linen

 fringed cloth d=clothing

 folded cloth? *gs*

 seal on necklace *ḫtm*, seal

 seal on necklace *ḫtmty*, seal bearer (a title)

 red crown *n*

 wall ornament *ẖkrt*, ornament or diadem

Signs based on strokes

| one stroke d=indicates ideogram

// two strokes *ỉ* or *y*

| | | three strokes d=plural

 three vertical strokes d=plural

Additional signs incorporating two sounds

Hieroglyph	Picture	Transliteration
	kiln	*t3*
	charcoal burner	*km*
 + 	cylinder seal?	*s3*
	fire swab	*sk*
	priest's staff?	*nḏ*
 + 	butcher's knife	*nm*

Hieroglyph	Picture	Transliteration
	twine on stick	*wd̲*
	net weaving tool	*ᶜd̲*
	black ibis	*gm*
	mortar carrier?	*ḳd*
	butcher's block	*h̲r*
	goat hide	*h̲n*
	rushes	*nn*
	throwing stick	*bḥ* or *ḥw*
	newborn calf	*i͗w*

APPENDIX B

How to calculate a date in the long count calendar

Let's say that you want to work out your birthdate in the Long Count Calendar. At first it appears complicated, but the system is logical when you have used it a time or two. Remember that the Long Count date is in days elapsed, starting on August 13, 3014 BC, and is measured in Baktuns, Katuns, Tuns, Unials, and Kins:

1 Kin	=		1 Day
20 Kins	=	Unial	(20 days)
18 Unials	=	Tun	(360 days)
20 Tuns	=	Katun	(7,200 days
20 Katuns	=	Baktun	(144,000 days)

The whole of the twentieth and the first part of the twenty-first centuries are in Baktun 12, so that part is easy: the first part of your date is 12. As an example, we'll work out the Maya date for a birthdate of October 20, 1944.

1. The first thing to notice is whether your birthdate year is a Leap-Year. 1944 is.
2. Next, work out how many days October 20 is into 1944.

   From the table we see that on October 1, 273 days have elapsed in a non-Leap Year, or 274 days in a Leap Year. Note that you only add the extra Leap Year day if you were born on February 29 or later in that year. Now add the 20 days since the beginning of October = 294 days since January 1st, 1944.

3 Next, divide 294 by 20 to see how many Unials are in 294 days. There are 14, with 14 days or Kins left over. This is written 14 14.
4 Now go to Table B to see what the January 1 Maya date was for 1944. We see that it was Baktun 12, Katun 16, Tun 10, Unial 0, Kin 5, written 12 16 10 0 5
5 We can now add the two together, placing Kin under Kin and Unial under Unial:

12	16	10	0	5
			14	14
12	16	10	14	19

Thus the Maya date for October 20, 1944 is Baktun 12, Katun 16, Tun 10, Unial 14, Kin 19. You can then turn the Arabic numbers into Maya numbers and fill in the blank hieroglyphic format which follows with this date.

This was a relatively easy Maya date. But say your birthday was December 29, 1931.

1 1931 was not a Leap-Year
2 On December 1, 334 days have elapsed. December 29 is 363 days into 1931. 363 divided by 20 is 19 Unials and 3 Kins. But there are only 18 Unials in a 360-day Tun, so 363 days = 1 Tun, O Unials, 3 Kins: 1 0 3.
3 The January 1 date for 1931 was 12 15 16 14 15.

12	15	16	14	15
		1	0	3
12	15	17	14	18

Thus, the only dates that will move into Tuns are those in late December: on or after December 26 in a non-Leap Year, and December 25 in a Leap Year.

There is one more situation to look at. Say you were born earlier in 1931, 12 Unials and 16 Kins into the year. Again, look at the January 1 date of 12 15 16 14 15. But now there is an addition problem:

12	15	16	14	15
			12	16
			26	31

There are only 20 Kins in a Unial, so the 31 is 1 Unial and 11 Kins. This now makes a total of 27 Unials. But, there are only 18 Unials in a Tun; 27 Unials = 1 Tun and 9 Unials. So, our correct date is 12 15 17 9 11. Again, this date can be transposed into Maya numbers and added to the blank format which follows.

Leap years

1912	1940	1968	1996
1916	1944	1972	2000
1920	1948	1976	2004
1924	1952	1980	2008
1928	1956	1984	2012
1932	1960	1988	
1936	1964	1992	

Table of days elapsed (since January 1)

1 Feb	31	1 August	212
1 March	59	1 September	243
1 April	90	1 October	273
1 May	120	1 November	304
1 June	151	1 December	334
1 July	181		

Table of January 1 Long Count dates (All are in Baktun 12)

Year	Katun	Tun	Unial	Kin	Year	Katun	Tun	Unial	Kin
1910	14	15	9	5	1946	16	12	0	16
1911	14	16	9	10	1947	16	13	1	1
1912	14	17	9	15	1948	16	14	1	6
1913	14	18	10	1	1949	16	15	1	12
1914	14	19	10	6	1950	16	16	1	17
1915	15	0	10	11	1951	16	17	2	2
1916	15	1	10	16	1952	16	18	2	7
1917	15	2	11	2	1953	16	19	2	13
1918	15	3	11	7	1954	17	0	2	18
1919	15	4	11	12	1955	17	1	3	3
1920	15	5	11	17	1956	17	2	3	8
1921	15	6	12	3	1957	17	3	3	14
1922	15	7	12	8	1958	17	4	3	19
1923	15	8	12	13	1959	17	5	4	4
1924	15	9	12	18	1960	17	6	4	9
1925	15	10	13	4	1961	17	7	4	15
1926	15	11	13	9	1962	17	8	5	0
1927	15	12	13	14	1963	17	9	5	5
1928	15	13	13	19	1964	17	10	5	10
1929	15	14	14	5	1965	17	11	5	16
1930	15	15	14	10	1966	17	12	6	1
1931	15	16	14	15	1967	17	13	6	6
1932	15	17	15	0	1968	17	14	6	11
1933	15	18	15	6	1969	17	15	6	17
1934	15	19	15	12	1970	17	16	7	2
1935	16	0	15	17	1971	17	17	7	7
1936	16	1	16	3	1972	17	18	7	12
1937	16	2	16	9	1973	17	19	7	18
1938	16	3	16	14	1974	18	0	8	3
1939	16	4	16	19	1975	18	1	8	8
1940	16	5	17	4	1976	18	2	8	13
1941	16	6	17	10	1977	18	3	8	19
1942	16	7	17	15	1978	18	4	9	4
1943	16	9	0	0	1979	18	5	9	9
1944	16	10	0	5	1980	18	6	9	14
1945	16	11	0	11	1981	18	7	10	0

Year	Katun	Tun	Unial	Kin	Year	Katun	Tun	Unial	Kin
1982	18	8	10	5	1998	19	4	14	9
1983	18	9	10	10	1999	19	5	14	14
1984	18	10	10	15	2000	19	6	14	19
1985	18	11	11	1	2001	19	7	15	5
1986	18	12	11	6	2002	19	8	15	10
1987	18	13	11	11	2003	19	9	15	15
1988	18	14	11	16	2004	19	10	16	0
1989	18	15	12	2	2005	19	11	16	6
1990	18	16	12	7	2006	19	12	16	11
1991	18	17	12	12	2007	19	13	16	16
1992	18	18	12	17	2008	19	14	17	1
1993	18	19	13	3	2009	19	15	17	7
1994	19	0	13	8	2010	19	16	17	12
1995	19	1	13	13	2011	19	17	17	17
1996	19	2	13	18	2012	19	19	0	2
1997	19	3	14	4					

KEY TO EXERCISES

Chapter 2

2.1 Gary

2.2 Charles (note that this and several of the following names are written phonetically, ignoring English spelling)

2.3 Patricia

2.4 Elizabeth

2.5 Martin

2.6 (the) old woman Susan (note that although the determinative is a male figure, it is actually without gender, and can be applied to a woman as well as a man)

2.7 (the) soldier Gregory or Gregory, the soldier

2.8 Sharon (is a real Egyptian name, one that has survived over 4,000 years)

2.9 (the King) Khufu (known to history more through his Greek name Cheops, he was supposedly the builder of the Great Pyramid)

2.10 (the Queen) Cleopatra (Cleopatra was a Greek who became queen after the Greek conquest of Egypt by Alexander the Great in the 4th century BC. Her name, like those of other Greek pharaohs, was translated phonetically)

2.11 (the King) Alexander

2.12 Caesar (Julius, Augustus, etc.) (Egypt was conquered by the Romans in the last years BC, and the names of Roman emporers were transliterated)

2.13 the god Sokar

2.14 the goddess Selket

Chapter 3

3.1 *ḏsr sḥ* (a or the) sacred shrine
3.2 *msʿ wr* great soldier
3.3 *ḏsr i͗b* (a or the) sacred heart
3.4 *nb wr pr* every great house
3.5 *wn mr* (the) light of love
3.6 *try sḥt* (a or the) keeper of the countryside
3.7 *ḏsr sḥ rʿ* (a or the) sacred shrine of the sun
3.8 *sr h3st* (an or the) official of the (or a) foreign land
3.9 *s3 k3* (the) son's ka (note the 'male' determinative is sometimes omitted)
3.10 *s3 rʿ* (the) Son of Ra or Re, a title of the pharaoh (note the 'male' determinative is usually omitted in this title)
3.11 *ḏsr i͗b w3 nṯr rʿ* (the) sacred heart of the great god Re (note this is not the usual positioning of the god's name, but it will suffice for the purpose of the exercise. There is more about this in Chapter 6).

Chapter 4

4.1 *ḫw nfr Rʿ stp* beautiful Khu, chosen of Ra (or Ra's chosen)
4.2 *s3t-sbk s3t=pr=snbi͗* Satsobek, daughter of the house of Senbi
4.3 *Ḫʿ=f-rʿ nb*=Heliopolis *wn=nwt* Khafre, Lord of Heliopolis, city of light
4.4 *snbi͗ rh nsw m-r pr b3k m3ʿ n st-i͗b=f* Senbi, king's advisor (and) overseer of the estate, true servant of his affection

Chapter 5

5.1 *ḥmt=i n* for my wife
5.2 *pr=f m* in his house
5.3 *b3k.nsw i͗n* by the servant of the king
5.4 *ḥmt=i͗ nb.t pr* my wife, (the) mistress of (the) house
5.5 *nn h3b=k s3=1 ḥnʿ b3k. nsw* you may not send my son with the servant of the king

Chapter 6

6.1 *ḥtp-dỉ-nsw 3sỉr nb ḏdw nb 3bḏw ḫnty-ỉmntw*

dỉ=f prt-ḫrw h3 t ḥnḳt ḫ3 k3 3pd ḫ3 mrḥt ḫ3 ḏf(3w)

w^{c}*b.t nfr.t nb.t ḫt* ^{c}*nḫt nṯr ỉm*

n k3 n ỉm3h(w) Sharon m3^{c}*-hrw*

An offering the king gives to Osiris, Lord of Dedju, Lord of Abydos, Khentyimentu

So that he may give a voice offering of a thousand (of) bread and beer, a thousand (of) ox and fowl, a thousand (of) oil, a thousand (of) provisions

Everything good and pure on which a god lives
For the ka of the venerable Sharon, true of voice

6.2 *rnpt-sp 22 ḫr ḥm nsw-bỉty Z n wsrt* ^{c}*nḫ ḏt r nḥḥ*

Regnal year 22 under the person of the King of Upper and Lower Egypt, Senwosret, living enduringly and repeatedly

6.3 *ỉ*^{c}*nhw tpw t3 is pn*

ḏd=tn h3 t ḥnḳt ḳbḥw nfr.t nb.t ḫt ỉm3h(w) nḫtỉ b3k m3^{c} *n st-ỉb=f m3*^{c}*-hrw*

O living upon the earth who may pass this tomb,
May you say a thousand (of) bread and beer, (a thousand of) libations, a (thousand of) every good thing (for) the revered one, the beloved servant, Nakhti, the justified

Chapter 8

8.1 51
8.2 100
8.3 174
8.4 200
8.5 241
8.6 318
8.7 399
8.8 baktun 8
katun 14
tun 3

unial 7
kin 15
12 Ben
6 Yaxkin
or 8 14 3 7 15 12   12 Ben 6 Yaxkin

8.9 baktun 8
katun 11
tun 9
unial 1
kin 17
or 8 11 9 1 17

8.10 baktun 9
katun 14
tun 17
unial 12
kin 10
10 Oc
5 Mol
or 9 14 17 12 10   10 Oc 5 Mol

FURTHER READING

Coe, Michael *The Maya*, (London: Thames and Hudson,1993).

Coe, Michael *Breaking the Maya Code*, (New York: Penguin, 1994).

Collier, Mark, and Manley, Bill *How to Read Egyptian Hieroglyphics*, (London: British Museum Press, 1998).

Davies, W.V. *Egyptian Hieroglyphics*, London: British Museum Press, 1987).

Henderson, John *The World of the Ancient Maya*, (London: John Murray, 1997).

Jacq, Christian *Fascinating Hieroglyphics* (New York: Sterling, 1998).

Kelly, David H. *Deciphering the Maya Script* (Austin: University of Texas Press, 1976).Morley, Sylvanus Griswold *An Introduction to the Study of Maya Hieroglyphics*, (New York: Dover Publications, 1975).

Speake, Graham Ed. *Atlas of Ancient Egypt*, (Oxford: Eqiunox, 1980).

Tompkins, Peter *Mysteries of the Mexican Pyramids*, (London: Thames and Hudson, 1987).

Zauzich, Karl-Theodore *Hieroglyphics*, (London: Thames and Hudson, 1992).

Encyclopedia Brittanica 'Hieroglyphics'

Also recommended:
The School for Scribes
Mark Collier and Bill Manley
PO Box 25020
Glasgow G1 5YD United Kingdom